DANIEL IONITA

Testament

ANTHOLOGY OF ROMANIAN VERSE

American Edition

IONITA, DANIEL

Testament - Anthology of Romanian Verse: Daniel Ionita; preface: Carmen Firan; foreword to
the second bilingual Romanian-English edition: Daniel Reynaud; foreword to the first bilingual
Romanian-English edition: Alex. Ştefănescu; editor: Daniel Ionita;
translators: Daniel Ionita, Eva Foster, Daniel Reynaud, Rochelle Bews

ISBN 978-0-9953502-0-5

I. Ştefănescu, Alex. (foreword to the first bilingual Ro/En edition)
II. Reynaud, Daniel (foreword to the second bilingual Ro/En edition)
III. Firan, Carmen (preface to the American edition)
IV. Ionita, Daniel (editor/principal translator)
V. Foster, Eva (translator)
VI. Reynaud, Daniel (translator)
VII. Rochelle Bews (translator)

This volume contains a large selection of poems translated by the authors for *Testament - Anthology of Modern Romanian Verse
- bilingual edition Romanian /English published by Minerva Publishing House in 2015*

DANIEL IONITA

Testament

ANTHOLOGY OF ROMANIAN VERSE

American Edition

Edited and translated by DANIEL IONITA

Assisted by Eva Foster, Daniel Reynaud

and Rochelle Bews

Sydney, 2016

Cover: Inspired from an original idea of Victoria Argint

Graphics: Cristina Dumitrescu

Editors: Cristina Drăgoi and Daniel Ionita

Corrections: Daniel Ionita, Rochelle Bews, Cristina Drăgoi,
                    Daniel Reynaud, Eva Foster

*For the love of poetry, which,
transcending culture and language,
reveals humanity's soul.*

Preface to the American edition

A Golden Dowry of Poetry

The word 'Testament' sounds ultimate and grave. It creates a kind of tension doubled by curiosity. Some are awaiting it with joy, hoping they will be included, others with the dread that they would be left out. Those who are not mentioned in the testament will never forgive you. Those you included may not forgive you either – because they expected more. The same applies to anthologies. Maybe this is why Daniel Ionita has chosen *Testament* as the title for his collection of Romanian poems in translation – a word which is both strong and challenging. Or maybe he took into consideration what we Romanians leave behind to English language readers of poetry, as well as to the generations of children of immigrants who, sooner or later, will want to know more about the place where their ancestors came from, about its poetry and the spirit of a space in which some buried their roots, and others transplanted them in a foreign soil.

Whatever the motivation, an anthology is a difficult undertaking, a complicated construction in which some are walled in so that others can fly, some have their wings burned and others have the sky open above them. Only the architect and the builder, both embodied in the anthologist, will know how much pain and work hide behind such an edifice which, if you are a creator yourself, can push your own projects back for a long time. As an author of anthologies myself,

carmen firan

of Romanian and American volumes, also published in the United States, I was in the shoes of he who raises resentment rather than gratitude, but that did not spoil my joy of giving something back to the Romanian literature which formed me.

There are not many comprehensive anthologies of Romanian poetry in English, and of those already published, there are few which stand out and are known. Daniel Ionita's *Testament – Anthology of Romanian Poetry,* now in its second edition, is a comprehensive volume, offering a panorama of reference for Romanian poetry, from the classics to the younger poets of today. The volume pays respect to the laws of consequence. No important name is forgotten. On the other hand, among the selected, there are lesser known authors, different voices, some unexpectedly fresh, which, by being associated with the masters, thus gain significance.

This present volume is conceived for the American space, with a selection of poets slightly different from the second edition, including some important poets who migrated to the United States (Ştefan Baciu, Nina Cassian, Liliana Sârbu, Nuţa Istrate Gangan, Adrian Sângeorzan, Carmen Firan) and Canada (Dumitru Ichim). Also, for this volume, the author has renounced the earlier bilingual versions and this anthology is published only in English. The poems are presented chronologically, in the order of the birth year of the poets: there are no bio sketches of the poets, there is no thematic grouping, the volume does not follow some literary current and the author does not follow current literary politics from Romania. It is a gesture of freedom and courage from a humanist dedicated to humanity, who, far from his country of birth, is planning for immortality through poems which marked his youth and sweetened his exile. *Testament* is not just a collection of poets and poems with documentary value; rather, it is an anthology with testamentary value! The poems are chosen by an idealist – a rare species these days

– an avid reader of poetry in general, and a lover of the beauty of the Romanian language in particular. Daniel Ionita appears as a late romantic with good taste, a stylist in love with musicality as such, a modern traditionalist who feels the need to save the dowry chest of the ancestors and to make it accessible in a large-currency language, English, firstly to the lovers of poetry conversant with it, but also to a future generation of migrants who at some stage will remember their Romanian roots, and that their parents and grandparents were reciting poems by Eminescu, Blaga, or Nichita Stănescu.

As mentioned, the poets are displayed in chronological order according to the year of birth, and therefore Mihai Eminescu, Romania's national poet, will appear second in the volume, after Vasile Alecsandri, for example. An English language reader will have to infer, almost without any other information of reference, the hierarchy of values. But ultimately what makes the value of a poem? Is it not the power of impression left on the reader? And here is the key success factor of this original collection – the quality of the translations. The great challenge for translators is to transpose into the target language not just the poem itself, but rather the emotions produced by it. The challenge is a lot bigger in the case of the present volume, as many of the selected poems are in the classical format, with rhyme, rhythm, and internal prosody.

The translations have fluidity, and often recreate the internal universe of the poem with inspired approaches. Daniel Ionita translates with his heart, as an authentic poet writes with his heart. Wherever you open this anthology you stumble upon, not just a particular poet, but upon a particular poem which might touch you, and you will feel like reading another one, and another… It is a dowry chest, and once you open its lid, you cannot stop from exploring what is inside: one of the great merits of this collection is the sensitivity of selection and the genuine form of joy in each verse.

carmen firan

11

You often hear the complaint that the appetite for poetry is diminishing. Some cry its demise on the background of a contemporary life full of stress, anxiety and lack of time. An increasingly colder world pushing rapidly towards the unforgiving mechanisms of surviving and success. But as runners in this race we need, everywhere and all the time, to reach the tranquility of an oasis, a refuge, a breath of fresh air. Poetry represents all of these. I trust in its force to withstand fear and darkness, to heal wounds, to feed empty souls, to satisfy the thirst of seekers for treasures of the spirit.

On another level, the poetry of a nation is equivalent to its testament, an emotional dowry, a concentrated history of relating to the reality of the ineffable over space and time. A mirror into the soul of a people, with all its reflections of light and shadow. It is said, not without ground, that poetry mirrors the seen and the unseen, the felt and inferred, transfiguring the exterior or interior world into words - artful, well-chosen words, or simple ones, but with an equal force of impression. Poetry is, more than anything, what remains after, or beyond, the words. A state of grace, a knot in the stomach, a tear lingering in the corner of the eye, something difficult to express… Poetry reflects its time and transcends it, condensing the essence of experience. It can transmit in a few words more emotion than scores of pages – sensations of the lightness of being, or those of Tenebrae. It is the wing of an angel, the energy of the earth, the thinness of the air, the song of the stars, a blow in the wind.

In *Testament,* Daniel Ionita offers the English language reader one such poetic experience. Not an anthology of names – rather a unique, superb selection of poetry, which synthesizes the identity of a national literature.

Carmen Firan
poet, novelist, translator and
Associate Editor at *Interpoezia* – New York

Foreword to the second bilingual
Romanian–English edition

Inside Romania's Soul

daniel reynaud

In the late 1970s, when I studied literature in Australia for my first degree, we covered the predictable territory for university literature courses of the era. There were the canonical texts of English literature: Chaucer, Shakespeare, Austen, Dickens, Wordsworth, T. S. Eliot and Bernard Shaw, along with many other British literary heavyweights. Then, of course, American literature with a sampling of Mark Twain, Robert Frost, Walt Whitman, and Steinbeck. And, being in Australia, there was naturally our own national literature, from the famed bush writers such as Henry Lawson and Banjo Paterson, through to Nobel-laureate Patrick White. There was even room to taste a bit of literature from across the Tasman Sea: one New Zealand novel was included in the course. Finally, there was a representation of great European works in translation.

While this was far from comprehensive, we were introduced to some French, German, Russian and even Norwegian writers: Camus, Goethe and Kafka, Tolstoy, Dostoevsky, Chekhov, and Ibsen, ensuring that we had some consciousness of the splendors of European literature.

Twelve years later I returned to the university scene as a lecturer. Things had changed. No self-respecting university would now overlook the important contributions of women writers, or of the many voices of postcolonial writing from Africa, India and south-east

Asia, the Middle East, the Pacific and the rest of the Americas. And much of this I taught. But in all of that, there were still gaps, still silences.

Enter one mildly obsessive literature fanatic exiled about as far as he could get from his native linguistic, cultural and literary roots. He was, in fact, a double exile, not just geographically but also professionally, into strange, remote fields such as Quality Assurance Management and Corporate Psychology. Yet his own passion kept him in touch with his distant homeland. Even in New Zealand and Australia, Daniel Ionita followed the latest writing emerging from "home" and longed for it to find a place in the new world in which he now lived.

So began Daniel's project to translate a representative selection of Romanian poetry into English, a project that eventually sucked me up into its path. He asked me to be involved in the later stages of the translation, hoping to ensure that the new linguistic clothes the poems wore would look good in English while still retaining their particular Romanian cut. With my French background (French was actually my first language), it was a delight to engage in the dialogue of trying to capture the romance of Latin-based poetry in its sturdy, functional Anglo-Saxon equivalent.

And in doing so, Daniel Ionita helped close a gap for me. Ostensibly schooled in the literature of the world, I knew virtually nothing of the literature of the European lands-in-between, those many little nations vulnerably wedged from north to south in a belt somewhere between Germany and Russia, and which escape the world's gaze except when someone shoots an Austrian Archduke in Bosnia, or invades Poland, or tries to reclaim "lost" borderlands, sparking another round of military conflagration.

And yet in those little nations, people are born, live and die through precisely the same set of experiences as we all do: glorious imagination and dull drudgery, sweetness and bitterness, triumph and tragedy. Indeed, perhaps they experience these things more intensely than many of us, for these nations have been subjected to some of the greatest highs and lows in human history, as the unfortunate meat in the sandwich of Great Power politics.

One of those "little" countries is Daniel's homeland, Romania. (I need to be careful when labelling other places "little": geographically, Romania is just a sliver of a country compared to Australia, yet its population just about equals that of my own vast but largely empty country. Throw in the Romanian diaspora from the borderlands, as well as Italy, Spain, France and the New World, and Romanian speakers easily match Australian numbers – so just what does "little" mean?)

Perched somewhat uncomfortably as the easternmost Latin outpost in a Slavic sea, and blessed with sun-drenched fertile plains and abundant oil, Romania has created poetry that holds the echoes of its history. Its origins were as a Roman colony guarding the imperial frontier against the barbarians who threatened to spill into Europe and claim its booty. It has felt the heel of virtually every invader of Europe since the fall of the Roman Empire: Germanic tribes, Huns, Slavs, and later the Mongolian Golden Horde and the Ottoman Turks left an imprint on the shattered population. Ruled by Slavs, Hungarians, Turks and Greeks, and having significant German-Saxon and Hungarian minorities, Romania has absorbed the flavors of them all. Just travel the nations surrounding Romania and sample their cuisine – then cross into Romania and eat again to savor the influences of a babel of cooking pots on the Romanian palate. And like its food, the Romanian language has absorbed words and expressions of Slavic, Hungarian, German, French, Italian, Turkish and Greek origin. Look into the faces and we see the genetic imprint of most of Europe and parts of Asia. And yet, and yet… it is still distinctively Romanian. Somehow this genetic melting-pot, these flavors, these cultural textures have been woven into a pattern that unmistakably cries out "Romania", even as we recognize the "otherness" of some of the influences.

And its poetry is that of a land that has known the tyranny of centuries of foreign oppressors, and the fleeting glories of medieval national independence with home-grown heroes such as Ștefan cel Mare (Stephen the Great), Mihai Viteazul (Michael the Great) and Vlad III Dracul (who entered western consciousness mediated through the propaganda of his enemies as Vlad the Impaler, the monstrous Dracula). And it has known its own native tyrannies as well, in the form of some of those same medieval heroes, and more recent despots, royalist, and Communist, who have added to the miseries of the people. In this politically constrained environment, a cultural renaissance, a Romanian Risorgimento, began in the early part of the 1800s, gradually throwing off the shackles of centuries of rule by the great empires that dominated their region: the Ottomans, Austria-Hungary, and Russia. Feeding nationalistic political aspirations was a revival of interest in Romanian language, literature, and culture.

The models were from fellow Latin countries, particularly France and Italy, and the renewed sense of Romanian-ness could be asserted against Turkish, Hungarian, and Russian hegemony. The alphabet was switched from the Cyrillic to the Roman, and a national literature was consciously cultivated as part of a broader Romanian art scene, which flourished into a corpus comparable with the best in any other national tradition.

Indeed, in the first half of the twentieth century, Romania could boast about two influential writers who led the world: poet Tristan Tzara, a founder of the Dadaist movement and, to a lesser extent, poet and playwright Eugen Ionescu (better known in the English-speaking world by his Frenchified name of Eugène Ionesco), a prominent figure of the Absurdist theatre. The particular luminosity of the nation's literary soul has been enriched by its own traumatic and glorious history, and its poets have drunk deeply from the wells of national anguish and bliss.

But can Romanian literature survive the latest and most aggressive form of cultural imperialism – that great devourer, the English language, which is invading the whole planet and gobbling up vulnerable cultures and languages? Yes! Resoundingly, yes. Romania's unique identity, founded in a brief century of Roman settlement, has survived the occupations and invasions of the better part of two millenia and has triumphantly reasserted itself in the modern era. Indeed, this volume that you are now holding is testament (sic!) to its resilience. By invading the invader, these poems proclaim their Romanian identity in the language of the imagined conqueror. In making the transition to English, these verses imprint themselves on the consciousness of the English-speaking world, reminding a potentially monolithic language that there are other resonances, other sensibilities, alive in the world that demand to be heard, that are too resistant to be swallowed up in English uniformity.

Hence, in my view, the importance of this volume: it brings that distinctive Romanian voice to the English language, helping us hear the Romanian accent through the English words of these poems. It is a bridge, or a gate, allowing Romania to make its presence felt in the new *lingua franca*, and at the same time giving English speakers access deep inside the Romanian soul. And, as always when we cross cultural boundaries, we find ourselves in an entirely-new-yet-strangely-familiar home. On the one hand, we sense a world of experiences that are common to all humanity. And yet, this world is presented to us with a voice that can only have come from the sum total of historical and cultural resonances that make Romania, Romania.

Associate Professor Daniel Reynaud
Avondale College of Higher Education –
New South Wales – Australia

daniel reynaud

Foreword to the first bilingual
Romanian-English edition

Poetry presented as a gift

alex. ştefănescu

There was a time when an anthology was an enthusiastic expression from an impassioned reader (sometimes a professional) who offered others the opportunity to read poems which had charmed him or her. These days an anthology is put together through the endeavor of literary critics in order to present their supreme authority before the public opinion; or perhaps through the restlessness of a new generation of poets striving to be noted, after having mercilessly purged previous currents.

To a great extent, the charm of those collections, compilations, and assemblages of the past has been lost. I almost feel like entreating our predecessors, overwhelmed by nostalgia like Eminescu in *Epigones:* "You were speaking holy riddles, lofty ideals you would fly;/ We just smear some waves on oceans, and with some stars we blotch the sky."

Daniel Ionita is perhaps one of the last romantics among anthology writers, due principally to his intent of representing Romanian poetry in English in an adequate and coherent manner. Established in Australia, in Sydney, and working in a field different from that of a literary professional, he continued to read Romanian poetry, as he did before he left his native country.

"The whole story of the translations"– explains Daniel Ionita –
"started in modest fashion. I intended to translate a few poems for my
children, my nephews and nieces, and other younger friends.
The common denominator for all of them was that, although they
could speak the Romanian language conversationally, they were
unable, I believe, to grasp the rare depth and beauty of its poetry – a
unique and varied pastel, a rich artistic voice among the great poetic
art of the world." How refreshing it would be if professional authors
of anthologies would display the same candor and good faith in their
endeavors! If they kept in mind, as a hypothetical intended audience
of the selected poems, their own children!

I would argue that the work of translation, which is in a way the work
of a literary critic, has shaped Daniel Ionita's aesthetic consciousness.
The most convincing argument for me is that he finalized this
anthology of modern Romanian poetry, *Testament*, with an
extraordinary effort, which simultaneously carried great pleasure.

The first thing you notice while going through the index summary
of the anthology is the innocent absence of the obligations which
specialists are burdened with, or at least think they are. The author
does not intend to illustrate some literary current or other, or to
include in this volume poems which might have just historical or
critical specialist value. His intentions are those of a butterfly flying
from flower to flower: to collect the sweetest and most beautifully
scented lyric nectar. His selection of poems, being unbiased by
specialization, is at the same time drastic. From every poet, the author
retains one single poem, rarely two, and in a few exceptional cases,
three. The poems are generally selected to be attractive from the first
reading. As such, they can be read in a live performance, can easily
be put to music, and above all, can be used to convince an English
language reader, who has perhaps never heard about Romania, to
pick up a Romanian poetry book and read from it.

The texts are organized in a chronological order reflecting the poets' birth years. Vasile Alecsandri, the first on the list, is represented through a well-known 'pastel', brimming with a joy easily transmitted to the reader: "From the sky the dreadful winter sifts and empties clouds of snow/ Of those cold and wandering snowdrifts having gathered long ago/ Snowflakes fly, they float and quiver like white butterflies, so light/ Spreading icy flutters, briskly, turn the country's shoulders white. /.../ But at once the snowing ceases, clouds depart, the sunny glow/ Glitters now, caressing gently the white ocean made of snow./ Look outside, for through the valleys a light sleigh is gliding fair/ And the joyful sky is ringing, play-bells chiming through the air." (*Winter*).

Eminescu follows (it is good that the author did not start with Eminescu, which would have been a conventional and unconvincing way of highlighting his value). From his poetry, Daniel Ionita selected, with a surefooted artistic instinct, the sonnet *Gone are the years*, and *Gloss*. The sonnet is essentially Eminescian, and at the same time, it presents the summative story of human life, in which everyone can find a reflection. In turn *Gloss* successfully transfers its metronome cadence into the English version: "Time is passing, time comes yet,/ All is old, and all is new;/ What for good or ill is set/ You can ponder and construe;/ Do not hope and do not worry,/ What's a wave, will wave away;/ Though enticing with a flurry /Cool remain to all they say."

Almost no important poet is missing. After Alecsandri and Eminescu, follow Alexandru Macedonski, George Coşbuc, Tudor Arghezi, Octavian Goga, Ion Minulescu, George Bacovia, Vasile Voiculescu, Ion Pillat, Ion Barbu, Lucian Blaga, Radu Gyr, Magda Isanos, Mihu Dragomir, Ştefan Augustin Doinaş, Ion Caraion, Irina Mavrodin, Nora Iuga, Mircea Ivănescu, Petre Stoica, Nichita Stănescu, Nicolae Labiş, Grigore Vieru, Marin Sorescu, Ileana Mălăncioiu,

Cezar Ivănescu, Ana Blandiana, Virgil Mazilescu, Adrian Păunescu, George Țărnea, Nicolae Dabija, Leo Butnaru, Leonida Lari, Liliana Ursu, Mircea Dinescu, Daniela Crăsnaru, Mircea Cărtărescu, Ioan Es. Pop, Lucian Vasilescu, Daniel Bănulescu, and a few other lesser known poets.

From Tudor Arghezi, the author selected, again in inspired fashion, the title poem *Testament*, from George Bacovia – *December* and *Lead*, from Ion Barbu – *King Crypto and the Lapp Enigel*, from Lucian Blaga – *I do not crush the crown of this world's wonders*, and *To waste is prone the month of May* and from Radu Gyr – *Rise up you Gheorghe, rise up you Ion*, and *Late last night, Jesus*.

Ștefan Augustin Doinaș is represented with (perhaps) his one-and-only poem written in a state of grace, *The silver-fanged boar*. Nichita Stănescu is present through two poems of abstract romanticism, very typical of him, *Moon in the field* and *Sentimental story*, and through one written in the jargon of his early years, *Ballad of the Tomcat*.

Daniel Ionita is very adept at selecting the poems: not just enchanting, but also quite translatable: "Later on we met more often. / I stood on one side of the hour, /you on the other, / like two handles of an amphora." and so on.

As I hoped, the anthology is not missing Nicolae Labiș. His poems, *Death of a dear* and *Dance*, written with spectacular talent, will delight, I am sure, the English readers. From Grigore Vieru I would have selected one or two of his emotionally charged poems on the theme of the mother; the author preferred *Bessarabia with sorrow*, representing Vieru as a *poeta vates* (a visionary poet), which is quite justified.

Apart from Nichita Stănescu, the sixties generation is represented in Daniel Ionita's anthology by poets who were, again, well chosen:

Marin Sorescu, Ileana Mălăncioiu, Cezar Ivănescu, Ana Blandiana, Virgil Mazilescu, Ioan Alexandru and Adrian Păunescu.

Being bilingual, the anthology will elicit interest, without a doubt, from Romanian readers as well, as it displays a pageant of modern Romanian poetry. It will be critiqued and contested, for sure, precisely because it does not consider literary politics as its fundamental rationale. However, it will be difficult to ignore.

Alex. Ștefănescu[*]

Editor's notes

Why and how?
The story of an anthology

daniel ionita

"There was nothing which could represent Romanian poetry on the world stage coherently, comprehensively, and with artistic and emotional equivalence – displaying all its beautiful complexity, in what is the lingua franca of today, the English language."

I use this opportunity of the American edition of *Testament* to reflect on the story of how this volume, in its various guises and editions, has come about. This might be of interest to some readers, whether amateurs or professionals. I will not be at all offended if the notes are ignored. The poems following them are far more interesting!

My journey leading to this volume started with a whim, progressing to a game, and then to an obsession – and all it took was a couple of careless steps. And then, a few years of some really hard work – about which no one warns you at the start. In the end, obsessive people have only themselves and their genes to blame for their condition. How else could I explain the manner in which one translated poem became 4, then 15, then 27, before I even became conscious that things had gone decidedly astray? By the time I had translated (or shall we say, reinterpreted?) 27 or 28 poems covering about 20 poets, I was beyond asking any existential questions: the current was too strong to swim back to shore. And so, here we have 147 poems, covering over 110 poets, and a period from halfway through the 19th century to the present day.

About seven years ago I translated a poem from Romanian into English and read it to a couple of people (he, an old-school, well educated bilingual Romanian in his late sixties, and she, a native English speaker) who became very emotional during the reciting. Thankfully not, as I feared initially, because of how bad the translation was. Apparently to the contrary.

The whole story started very modestly: my goal was to translate a few poems for my children, my nephews and nieces, and a few other younger friends. Born outside Romania, or at least having grown up and been educated elsewhere, they could not appreciate Romanian poetry or Romanian literature. As a common denominator, they had a conversational understanding of Romanian, but they were unable to 'taste' Romanian poetry. They were unable, I believe, to grasp its rare depth and beauty – a unique, though pastel-varied, artistic voice among the great poetic art of the world.

Later when the poem (Octavian Goga's *Song IV – To you the wind may pay a visit*) was read by its intended audience, my children, the reaction was less emotional, their casual "That was nice", morphed into "That is very nice, Dad", when my countenance became stern all of a sudden...

An avid consumer of literature in general, I have spent most of my life in English speaking countries, becoming familiar with English language literature, classical and contemporary, but also maintaining an interest in the literature of my country of birth, Romania. I have always felt the pangs of regret that my children would not get to discover the rich spiritual artistic soul of their parents' country.

I guess this must be a common feeling among first generation migrants, which necessarily, and thankfully probably, diminishes in their children.

Having said that, my eldest daughter, a high school English teacher, had read a couple of novels and works translated into English – *Dishevelled Maidens* by Hortensia Papadat-Bengescu, and *Tales from Ancuţa's Inn* by Mihail Sadoveanu – which she liked. But that was that, as far as Romanian literature was concerned, and, in a sad indictment, I was not able to source other Romanian novels in English.

The situation with Romanian poetry was similar. There were a few gems, starting with the integral translation of Mihai Eminescu by the hugely talented Corneliu M. Popescu. A measure of his talent can be seen in that the English Poetry Society named its Prize for poetry translations into English after the young Romanian translator's name. Popescu died aged 19, on the tragic evening of 4 March 1977, in an earthquake which took a number of artists, singers, actors, who happened to live in some of the stylishly bohemian, but old and shabby buildings of central Bucharest.

Elsewhere, there are a few good translations of poets who have found their home overseas, especially in the USA, such as Ion Caraion, Nina Cassian and Liliana Ursu. Adam Sorkin, in conjunction with Lidia Vianu and others, has come up with noteworthy translations of Marin Sorescu and Nichita Stănescu, for example, attempting to access the subtle and beautiful flavor of the original Romanian works.

Apart from that, I found quite a number of translations of average quality and an even larger number at an embarrassing level. I shall not follow this path of discussion too far; being a translator myself – as I am well aware of the very apt English proverb about people living in glass houses…

daniel ionita

The main issue, though – which was pointed out to me by the extremely erudite Ana Munteanu, chief-editor of the Romanian edition of this work at Minerva Publishing House – was that there was no comprehensive representation of Romanian poetry in English. Therefore, I owe Ana Munteanu the vision of creating an anthology, rather than just "Daniel Ionita's collection of favourite poems". What we had, until this work was published, were either translations of single poets, or, at best, of a group of poets representing an era, or a particular current. There was nothing which could represent Romanian poetry on the world stage coherently, comprehensively, and with artistic and emotional equivalence – displaying all its beautiful complexity, in what is the *lingua franca* of today, the English language.

This interaction with Ana Munteanu moved me from my modest quest to translate "a few" poems, to the emergence of this anthology. I am not even sure what "a few" meant, in my self-talk, at the time. Maybe four, five... At least this was my rationalization some two years after I started translating (maybe in 2012), when finishing the first draft of Mircea Cărtărescu's free-verse *I am smiling,* and starting the constraining but hauntingly beautiful form of Eminescu's *Gone are the years,* a straight-jacket Petrarchan-style sonnet.

A bridge which helped me to start crossing the divide to English was formed by poems put to music. Since my children have been exposed over the years to Romanian folk music, it was only natural that my first attempts covered poems by authors like Octavian Goga, Nichita Stănescu, Ana Blandiana, George Țărnea, or Adrian Păunescu, whose works have been put to song for a number of decades. Their established musicality and rhythm were very helpful for translation.

daniel ionita

A short side-track here… After leaving Romania in 1980, we settled
for the first 10 years in Auckland, New Zealand, far removed from
anything cultural, be it music or poetry, from Romania – in the days
without internet with its Facebook, YouTube, Spotify and other
marvels of connectivity and distribution, which we take for granted
these days (yes, such a world did exist!). One of the very few things
that kept me linked to great Romanian poetry, were the verses put
to music by great singer-songwriters such as Nicu Alifantis, Mircea
Baniciu, Adrian Ivaniţchi, Cătălin Condurache, Mircea Vintilă,
Tatiana Stepa, Mădălina Amon, Ştefan Hruşcă, Ducu Berţi, Anda
Călugăreanu, Margareta Pâslaru and others, whose tapes and LPs
managed to make their way, rarely, but crucially, via friends and
relatives, from Romania all the way to New Zealand. I am deeply
indebted to all these artists, as well as to their mentor and discoverer,
the great poet and promoter Adrian Păunescu. I know, Păunescu
is often labelled as a stooge of the communist regime, and I do not
necessarily subscribe to his political views – though some argue that
he was a real patriot who undermined the regime from the inside.
Be that as it may, from my perspective were it not for the vision,
energy and enthusiasm of Adrian Păunescu and the Flacăra (Flame)
cultural mega-events he organized for about a decade – from the
mid-seventies until stopped by the Ceauşescu regime in 1986 – I,
in faraway New Zealand and then Australia, might have forever lost
my connection with Romanian culture and especially poetry. For it
was through these forums, and with the specific encouragement and
mentoring of Adrian Păunescu, that artists such as those mentioned
above created their marvelous work, in the midst of one of the most
severe Communist regimes in Eastern Europe. And now let us get
back to the main trail…

Various individuals questioned, at times, the reasons and validity of
this kind of work and advised me not to proceed. Arguments began

with "Who cares about Romanian poetry – Romanians even don't care anymore! Outside Romania?... no one cares..." (This struck me as an obvious and gross exaggeration, if not an outright lie, because here was I, at least one person who cared!)

Others told me amiably that they had seen translations made by "sentimental immigrants" (sic!) and were not all that impressed. I could not disagree entirely with this argument, for the reasons already alluded to above, revealed by my own research regarding poetry translations from Romanian into English. But I do not believe this is an argument to be put against all translations.
Finally, others insisted with the argument that "poetry cannot be translated, it needs to be read in the original". I disagree with this view, as you might expect. One of the first 'trolls' on the subject was Robert Frost with his famous, and most likely whimsical, "poetry is what is left out of translation" – meaning that poems can only be read in the original language, therefore rendering every translation fake. However, the evidence against this argument is straightforward, as well as being overwhelming: Shakespeare, Yates, Frost himself, Baudelaire, Verlaine, Hugo, Whitman, Browning, Cummins, Heine, Rilke, Pushkin, Lermontov, Esenin, de Vega, Tasso, Petrarch, Omar Khayyam, Rabindranath Tagore, and shifting a lot earlier to biblical poetry writing – Psalms, Book of Job, The Song of Songs, or the likes of Homer, Vergil, Ovid, all of them representatives of great poetry, have been translated. As a result, they have entered universal consciousness. Hence, my belief that translation of poetry can be carried out faithfully and meaningfully.

On the other hand, I partially agree with the Italian proverb "traduttore… traditore": the translator is a traitor. For, in order to cross the long and very narrow foot-bridge launched over the abyss between two languages, two cultures, two ways of thinking and feeling, there is an acute need for compromise, for interpretation and re-imagining.

daniel ionita

The translator enters what is essentially a Faustian pact. For, as Associate Professor Daniel Reynaud said to me at the beginning of my editing and translating journey, there is no such thing as poetry translation. (Later, I discovered this view is common – and common sense – among researchers and theorists of poetry translation.)

There is only poetry reinterpreted in a different language. The eternal problem for the translator or, more correctly, the re-interpreter, resides in the constant choices which arise when transferring a poem from the source language and culture to the target ones. Naturally many words do not have a one-to-one correspondence across languages, and so the translator is forced into compromise. And poetry, that most intense and condensed form of language, is where these compromises have the hardest impact. Even the most basic elements, such as poetic form – rhythm and rhyme for example – are no trivial matter. That is because different languages can have different prosodies or internal musical rhythms. Add to that the complexities of imagery, mood, diction and voice, and it is little surprise that translators shy away from poetry, or that those foolish enough to start this fraught journey end up badly.

How does one capture the simultaneous effects of a poetic image, with its inter-tangled meanings generated through denotation and connotation – some of which are culturally loaded, like puns and metaphor, thus particularly resistant to translation? How does one then mix this in with the above mentioned prosody, rhythm, rhyme? These problems only multiply as one works with whole lines, stanzas, poems, styles, genres, poetic eras.

But perhaps the biggest issue challenging the re-interpreter of poems into English, especially from Romance languages, has been well documented: it relates to prosody, and the use, or misuse – as the case might be – of supplementing words into the English version. Why do we need this supplementation, or padding up? Because "high

daniel ionita

mileage" poetic terms such as those representing emotions (love, joy, pain), nature elements (sun, moon, creek, tree), or body elements (eyes, hand, foot, heart) are monosyllabic in the English language, while being anything but in Romanian: iu-bi-re, bu-cu-ri-e, du-re-re, soa-re, lu-nă, pâ-râu, co-pac, mâ-nă, pi-cior, i-ni-mă. This goes for other Latin-based languages too.

Hence, the same verse in English will necessarily contain more words than in the original Romanian, simply to maintain the number of syllables, the rhythm – that is to make equivalent the original feel of the poem in Romanian to the prosody of English. To the translator, this issue, specific to the boundary of Romance languages and English, is both a blessing and a curse, for obvious reasons: you have more room to add extra words to help the rhythm and the rhyme.

However, this 'padding up' or supplementing, can be a fraught exercise: one can easily supplement distracting, irrelevant or simply un-poetic garbage.

A good translation, however, does remain as faithful as possible to the original and not just in a simple transactional sense. For me, the best definitions of 'faithfulness' in poetry translation, and the ones which I espoused for the present work, are provided by Jonas Zdanys – to strive for emotional equivalence, rather than one-for-one transactional precision – and by Roman Jakobson, some decades ago: to be faithful, the re-interpretation needs to balance [the holy trinity of] aesthetics, semantics, and form.

Unfortunately, the approach currently fashionable with poetry translation academics in the "western school", dictates that the translation stays as closely as possible to the original semantic, to the detriment, if need be, of prosody, of feel. Needless to say, this is an approach I broadly discarded – I found its clamor for precision-at-any-cost, at best misguided, but mostly abhorrent.

To me, authenticity, or faithfulness – as well-recognized translation theorists and practitioners like Peter Robinson and A. K. Ramanujan put it – has a lot to do with the broad sense and feel of the poem: not just the semantic, but also the philosophical, as well as the artistic expression of the poetic idea, with texture, color, rhythm, flow and musicality. The principle which governed my translation process was to strive towards reproducing in English, as closely as possible, the overall intellectual and emotional impact of the poem in its original Romanian. To do this meant being willing to make every element of poetics subservient to this guiding principle. At times, for example, transactionally different, but poetically equivalent, English language images have been substituted for the original Romanian, while attempting to keep the overall meaning, the prosody and, of course, the rhyme in most cases, where applicable. My primary concern, as you might expect, was that the poems cross well, and flow well, in the translated version.

Perhaps the most interesting challenge was how to render the original stylistic features into their English equivalents. Many of the older Romanian writers used a poetic form of Romanian – with vocabulary, phrases, and rhymes which pushed the boundaries of everyday Romanian, similar perhaps to the poetic conventions common in much of the English poetry pre-1900. Thankfully a majority of the translations in this volume deal with modern and contemporary, post-1900 poets, where these specific challenges are less present.

Editorial Choices

While over 100 poets and 140 odd poems may sound comprehensive in anyone's language (…), I am sure there will be those who will find that I've missed some favorite poet of theirs, or (more likely) will be asking why I included another. I have already been questioned as to

daniel ionita

why some early, pre-1800 poets are not included – the implication being that, therefore, this anthology might not be representative. My answer is that I never intended to write a historical anthology covering all periods of Romanian poetry, and initially at least, I did not feel responsible for doing so. My first question always was: do I like the poem I am including here?

Secondly: do I think it will carry well in English? However, a possible future edition might well include pre-nineteenth century works such as Dosoftei's *Psalter,* or Ienăchiţă Văcărescu's early attempts at poetry in the Romanian language.
The works included in this anthology can be divided into three broad categories, none of them easily definable or fully agreed upon by experts: the "classics", the consecrated contemporaries, and my own "gut feel" choices of lesser known poets.

One thing is certain. This collection of poems is not carried out from a literary critic's perspective. Sure, having to read lots of poems in order to make decisions, educates one to be somewhat of a critic. However, I have chosen poems more from a "consumer's perspective", if you like.

Therefore, my rationale for choosing particular poets to be represented here, and more importantly, particular poems, had little to do with usual literary analysis. I did not choose poems significant for some important historical or stylistic shift, or representative for some technical particularity. Rather, as literary historian Alex. Ştefănescu observed in his foreword to an earlier, bilingual edition, I have chosen the poems which would carry well into the target language and culture: "… like a butterfly hopping from flower to flower, Daniel Ionita has chosen the sweetest nectar of Romanian poetry… poems which [have a chance] to convince the English language reader to pick up and read Romanian literature".

daniel ionita

Having said this, Romanians will recognize in this volume quite a few classical (in the sense of highly regarded) poems, selected by literary specialists to be taught in Romanian literature classes throughout high school and university. These works have picked themselves, and I hope the English-speaking reader will agree.

Speaking of 'the classics', the reason for their inclusion was not just for historical-literary reasons, nor simply for a sense of duty. First, it was because they wrote some sensational poetry, hence their labeling by most critics as 'classics'. Secondly, I intended to give the reader unfamiliar with Romanian poetry a feel for its broader contextual pedigree. Works by earlier, nineteenth century born, poets such as Vasile Alecsandri, Mihai Eminescu, George Coşbuc, Alexandru Macedonski, Ion Minulescu, George Bacovia, Octavian Goga, Tudor Arghezi, George Topîrceanu, Ion Barbu, Magda Isanos or Lucian Blaga, would help the foreign reader better grasp the artistic evolution of Romanian poetry. This, in turn, will hopefully lead to a better insight and enjoyment of the modern and contemporary poets, whom this volume mostly covers.

In relation to contemporary 'classics', the generation of poets who became well known in the decades from 1950 through to 1970, few Romanian critics would argue with the presence of Nicolae Labiş, Nichita Stănescu, Nina Cassian, Marin Sorescu, Nora Iuga, Ioan Alexandru, Adrian Păunescu, Ana Blandiana, Mircea Dinescu, Leonid Dimov, George Ţărnea, or Romulus Vulpescu. However, in regards to the poets who became consecrated after this period, I needed and thankfully received some extremely useful help.

That is because, having left Romania in 1980 at twenty years of age and in a time when world connectivity was still some 15 years away, I lost touch with the developments of poetry in my country of origin, especially after the fall of the Ceaușescu regime in 1989. Of immense help to me here, have been a) the exceptional literary pedigree of Ana Munteanu, chief-editor at Minerva Publishing House, who produced for me the earlier bilingual editions of this anthology, b)the immense generosity of my good friend and literary critic Alex. Ștefănescu, and c) the precise insight and advice from Nicolae Manolescu, noted literary critic and (at the time of the publishing of this volume) president of the Writers Union of Romania. More of them later.

At this juncture it suffices to say that through them, I came to know and include in here exceptional poets such as Adrian Popescu, Ioan Es. Pop, Daniel Bănulescu, Ion Stratan, Aurel Rău, Emil Brumaru, Cezar Ivănescu, Daniel Bănulescu, Florin Iaru, Horia Bădescu, Mihaela Malea Stroe, Ileana Mălăncioiu, Lucian Vasilescu, Marta Petreu and many others.

A third category, a small one, is that of the lesser known poets. Some of them I consider up-and-coming (and here I take the risk and feel the buzz of the 'discoverer') while others will never make it to the bigger stage. However, I chose to include them, simply because I like their poetry, perhaps the particular chosen poem. Admittedly, this is an indulgence for which I might be chastised… but poetry has never been, and hopefully will never become a predominantly left-brain, rational activity. Some level of subjectivity will, hopefully, forever remain.

One particular group of poets, peppered through the volume, is that of Romanian-language poets born in what is currently the Republic of Moldova. This has been done not simply as a political move, though I deliberately wanted to send a signal that Romanian-language writers from the former Soviet space are not forgotten. However, I am also convinced that their selection stands up to scrutiny on poetic grounds: Grigore Vieru, Leonida Lari, Leo Butnaru, Dumitru Băluță, Arcadie Suceveanu, Arhip Cibotaru, Nicolae Dabija, Renata Verejanu and a few others.

There were a couple of pieces of advice received, which I have chosen to ignore, probably to my peril, but "qui ne risque rien, ne gagne rien" as the French proverb goes. One suggestion was in relation to poets who might have praised the communist regime through their art – and therefore might morally "taint" this anthology, in some people's opinion. Some important and less important literary representatives winced or even chastised me vehemently – sometimes in print – when they noticed, in the volume, names such as Adrian Păunescu, Mihu Dragomir, Eugen Evu, Mihai Beniuc, Miron Radu Paraschivescu – poets accused "to have sold out" politically, when others chose to risk not being published, rather than compromise with the totalitarian regime between 1947 and 1989. The question of the skeptics was: how can you include compromised or controversial names as those above, alongside martyrs like Vasile Voiculescu or Radu Gyr, who suffered long years of imprisonment and torture during the Stalinist period (1947- 1964)? While controversy will reign on this subject for a long time, my approach was to consider the poets simply in their role as artists and to make a judgment simply regarding their poetic talent. To take my position to an extreme, should Nicolae Ceaușescu himself have written some good poetry, I would have included him in this anthology. Luckily for me and my critics on this matter, while he was praised for being multi-talented to the point of omniscience, Ceaușescu never dabbled in poetry!

On the more serious side, my view coincides with the opinion expressed by Alex. Ștefănescu, that writers such as those mentioned above were themselves victims of that regime, stifled and torn in many ways – and should be, perhaps, more pitied than blamed. Secondly, some people raised an eyebrow at the presence of some poets, Ștefan Augustin Doinaș comes to mind, who only ever produced one or two outstanding poems, the rest of their work being mediocre, or so the consensus goes. To stick to Doinaș, my argument is that his one outstanding poem, *The silver-fanged boar,* is such an amazingly bright diamond of Romanian poetry – on a par with anything Eminescu or Nichita Stănescu might have written, that it warrants being represented here. Certainly, Eminescu, Arghezi, Blandiana, Stănescu, Păunescu, Voiculescu and others, might have had a lot more "hits" – and that is reflected by their representation with more than one single poem in this volume.

Thanks

Three people have been most helpful to me regarding this volume: my linguistics specialists Eva Foster, Associate Professor Daniel Reynaud (Avondale College of Higher Education), and Rochelle Bews. Before even reading Peter Robinson, I instinctively followed the view that poet-translators (such as me) should seek help from linguists, rather than other poets. The contribution of my linguist colleagues on, for example, expression, rhythm, and even some rhyming issues, was decisive in making this work a superior endeavor.

I must mention at this point the noted Australian poet and lecturer in Creative Writing (University of Sydney), Judith Beveridge, who generously contributed her time and poetic sense to one of my early attempts at this work: her recommendations had an important influence on my approach.

Second come the group of people – some of them already mentioned – who influenced the selection of some of the poets represented here. The most important among these is Ana Munteanu. (To give a contextual idea of her literary pedigree, Ms. Munteanu is the daughter of the late great comparative-literature professor and publisher Romul Munteanu, who managed to translate and publish important contemporary western literature during the repressive years of the Ceaușescu regime. He did this through sheer courage

daniel ionita

44

and determination, as well as using the weight of his professional standing, both in Romania and abroad. He is credited with singlehandedly managing to keep Romanian writers and critics informed about key literary developments outside the insular world of Communism.) Ms. Munteanu provided both the erudition and the relationships I needed in order to get to know important contemporary poets, whom I might have otherwise overlooked.

Because of her own publishing work as chief-editor at Minerva Publishing House, the oldest continually functioning publisher in Romania, and one of the most prestigious, she commands a lot of respect in Romania's literary circles, and therefore important doors opened to me following a simple email or phone call from her.

The second person in this category of influencers is literary critic and historian Alex. Ştefănescu. His standing in Romanian literary history is beyond question since the publishing of his *History of Romanian Literature 1940-2000*, which answers the fraught question of what happened to Romanian literature during the communist era. Since the release of the first edition of *Testament – Anthology of Modern Romanian Verse* (bilingual version) in 2012, Alex has been a continuous source of inspiration and knowledge, always willing to help with advice and constructive critique. While his erudition is beyond question, what I appreciated most is his enthusiasm, sense of humor, and amazing insight into the artistic, but also the human aspects of key contemporary literary figures in Romania.
Through the good grace of Dr. Floricel Mocanu, Consul General of Romania in Sydney, himself a literary specialist and translator, I was put in touch with the other great contemporary literary historian, Nicolae Manolescu, president of the Romanian Writers Union.

Despite his busy schedule (he was also, at the time, Romania's ambassador to UNESCO in Paris) Mr. Manolescu was very graceful in taking the time to give his opinion on my choices.

daniel ionita

It is important to mention, I believe, that I never felt any of these key mentors ever trying to impose their considerably educated views. Rather, I always felt I had full editorial freedom, and I enjoyed their respect, as an anthologist, even when we disagreed.

Dr. Mocanu, mentioned earlier, deserves an additional mention, not just because he suggested three of the poets represented here (Alexandru Muşina, Dinu Olăraşu, and Miron Radu Paraschivescu), but also because of his enthusiastic support for the earlier bilingual editions forming the basis for the current volume, as well as for my own poetry work in general – which he helped promote here in Sydney.

Others who had a key influence on the shape of this volume were my good friends, the singer-songwriters Nicu Alifantis, Adrian Ivaniţchi and Cătălin Condurache. Not only did they provide, unwittingly initially, the spark for me to start translating (my first translated poems were some of those used by them for their beautiful songs), but they have also supported me with my various book launches, whether for anthologies or my own original work. In addition, Cătălin Condurache also encouraged me to become familiar with the important literary movement Echinox from Cluj, through which I got to know and love the poetry of Adrian Popescu, Horia Bădescu, Marta Petreu, Ion Pop, Vasile Igna, and Aurel Rău. Adrian Ivaniţchi became such an enthusiastic supporter of my endeavors, that he gifted to me a great part of his amazing collection of poetry! Together with Nicu Alifantis, he also pressed me to become familiar with the works of some great poets such as Constanţa Buzea, Leonid Dimov, or Romulus Vulpescu, for which I will forever be grateful.

My family had a great influence on the creation of this work. Starting with my children, who provided the spark for this volume, and who, I hope, will read it. Then there are my parents, who provided both the DNA and the milieu conducive to the appreciation of poetry – our bookshelves in suburban Bucharest contained most of the great Romanian poetry and prose, as well as a good representation of German, French, British, American and Russian volumes.

My mother, Rodica, has a natural as well as an educated poetic and linguistic sense, most likely inherited from my grandfather Ioan Ogrean, who was somewhat of a "bush-poet", to use an apt Australian expression, an amateur who occasionally wrote poems for private and family enjoyment. My mother could easily recite Heine, Rilke or Lermontov in German and Russian, respectively, and still does it now, at 80 years of age. On the other side of the family, my father Constantin, my aunt Elena, and my uncle Marin provided me with regular poetry recitals during my early years, especially poetry with spiritual underpinnings.

And last, but never ever least, there is my wife, Nicoleta Luminița, who has constantly encouraged and supported me. As you might imagine, as I also have a "day job", the amount of work required by this anthology encroached into family and leisure time. My wife's sustained support, her understanding of my 'obsession' and her appreciation of the work at an artistic level, as well as the occasional sharp critique (only when specifically asked – thankfully!), hold immeasurable value.

Daniel Ionita
Sydney – Australia, July 2016

Testament

Anthology of Romanian Verse

American Edition

From the sky, the dreadful winter sifts and empties clouds of snow,

Of those cold and wandering snowdrifts having gathered long ago;

Snowflakes fly, they float and quiver like white butterflies, so light,

Spreading icy flutters, briskly, turn the country's shoulders white.

mountains

Days are snowing, nights are snowing, snow on mornings does prevail!

All the countryside is wearing, regally, this silver mail;

chain mail

And the sun, all round and pale, shows but glimpses through the sky,

Like some dream of youth, now flashing through the years which pass us by.

All is white... the fields, the hillsides, all surrounding, far away,

Like white daydreams are the poplars, lining up into the grey,

tree species — tall, narrow, and fast-growing

And beholding all this wasteland, not a trail, not a stroke,

Just the villages, now hidden under whitish foam of smoke.

But at once the snowing ceases, clouds depart, the sunny glow

Glitters now, caressing gently the white ocean made of snow.

Look outside, for through the valleys, a light sleigh is gliding fair…

And the joyful sky is ringing, play-bells chiming through the air.

50

gone are the years

Gone are the years, long clouds across the plain
And never will I witness them return,
They charmed me then, but I no longer yearn
For tales and doinas*, riddles all in vain,

Where childhood thoughts would joyfully abide
Barely discerned, now full of deep discerning –
For your cool shadows, I'm no longer burning,
Oh, time of mystery, at the even tide!

To tear some sound from life forever passed,
To try, my soul, for you again to quiver
In vain my hand across the strings is skimming;
The gleam of youth, away, forever cast,
Spent, the sweet murmur that would once deliver,
While now, time grows behind me... I am dimming!

mihai eminescu

1850–1889

---

* **Doina** – a Romanian musical style, found in peasant music, often melancholy, typically not constrained by a particular rhythm, and often varied according to the interpreter's mood and imagination.

gloss

Time is passing, time comes yet,
All is old, and all is new;
What for good or ill is set
You can ponder and construe;
Do not hope and do not worry,
What's a wave, will wave away;
Though enticing with a flurry,
Cool remain to all they say.

Many things pass by before us,
Many things we hear and see,
Who remembers all their ruckus
And would listen to their plea?…
You sit calmly 'round the edges,
Find yourself, despite their threat,
While you hear their noisy pledges,
Time is passing, time comes yet.

Not inclining in expression
The cold balance of our thinking
To a moment, an impression,
Mask of happiness now sinking,
Of its own death notwithstanding
Takes one lonely breath for you;
But for him who's understanding
All is old, and all is new.

Entertained by actors playing
In this world yourself depict:
Though four roles one is portraying,
His true face you can predict;
If he weeps, or if he's fighting,
You just watch him without fret
And deduce from his inciting
What for good or ill is set.

Past and future go together,
The two faces of a coin,
You can tell tomorrow's weather,
Then you learn the two to join;
All that was and all that follows
In this moment we see true,
On their false and empty hollows
You can ponder and construe

The same means this world is using
To constrain in all she fashions,
And for thousand years suffusing
Joy and sadness duly rations;
Other masks, the same old drama,
Other mouths, the same old story,
Discontent at their conformance
Do not hope and do not worry.

Do not hope because some cretin
Wrestles to successes steady,
Idiots will have you beaten,
Though you've shown them off already;
Have no fear if when they gather
Ostentations they display,
Don't resemble them, don't blather:
What's a wave, will wave away.

Like some charming siren calling,
The world's luring and inviting;
Other actors when they're falling,
It wants you to do their fighting;
Move aside, it's just deception,
Pass them by, away you scurry,
From your path make no exception,
Though enticing with a flurry.

Should they touch you, get some distance,
Should they curse you, keep your polish,
Why advise and show persistence,
When you know they just demolish?
Let them blather on forever,
Doesn't matter whom they sway,
Don't grow fond of them, be clever,
Cool remain to all they say.

Cool remain to all they say,
Though enticing with a flurry;
What's a wave, will wave away,
Do not hope and do not worry;
You can ponder and construe
What for good or ill is set;
All is old, and all is new:
Times is passing, time comes yet.

1850–1889 mihai eminescu

why won't you come

See how the swallows flee our town,
Dead walnut leaves are shaken down,
The vineyard's frosty now, and glum –
Why won't you come, why won't you come?

Pray fall again in my embrace,
And ardent I'll behold your face,
I'd sweetly lay my head to rest,
Upon your breast, upon your breast!

Remember how in times gone by,
We walked together, you and I,
I'd lift you up into my arms
So many times, so many times!

The world is full of lovely girls
With fiery eyes which shine like pearls
But be they angels to my view,
They are not you, they are not you!

You brighten up my day and night
And take my soul to sweet delight,
Beside you, stars have lost their sheen,
My lovely queen, my lovely queen!

Late autumn now arises gray,
Dead leaves are falling in our way,
The meadows play a sad old strum...
Why won't you come, why won't you come?

mihai eminescu

1850–1889

rondel of the dying roses

1854–1920 alexandru macedonski

It's time for roses now to die.
They die in gardens, die in me.
So full of life they were, you see,
But now they go without a sigh.

A shudder climbs into the sky.
Deep sorrow reaches every plea.
It's time for roses now to die –
They die in gardens, die in me.

Beneath the evening's mournful cry
Chaotic sobs rise in a spree,
Deep through the night that is to be
Their heads in tender peace they lie...
It's time for roses now to die.

Decebalus* to his people

This life's a stale and aimless jaunt
If you don't live as is your wont!
A tyrant tribe demands with blare,
Around your neck a yoke to wear:
We're born and that's a cursed haunt,
        Do we wish a second snare?

For even if to gods we're heir,
One death is all we're asked to bear!
It's all the same should you have died
When young, or old from life you slide;
But not the same a dog to die,
        Or lion in your stride.

Those who go fighting with a whine,
Even if battling first in line,
No better are they in our sight
Than cowards who have turned to white!
For if to whining you resign,
        Your cry's a vain recite!

george coşbuc

1866–1918

---

* **Decebalus** was a Dacian king who defied successive Roman emperors in order to maintain the independence of his country. Finally defeated, he committed suicide rather than be humiliated by his conquerors.

For to keep still the cowards strive!
All dead are still, but who's alive
Laugh loudly! Good ones laugh and die!
Let us then laugh, brave men, let's fly
In roaring laughter. Thus, we thrive
   And hell to heaven tie!

And if the blood would flow a spring,
Your arm shall undefeated swing
When fear of death you won't allow!
For like a god, you never bow,
But laugh at the worst fears that wring
   And stun your strongest foe.

For they are Romans! Such a deal!
Not them, but if Zalmoxis' will,
With his whole host of gods, descend,
We'll ask them what they want,
And send them back; this land's our till,
   The heavens they can tend!

1866–1918   george coşbuc

---

* **Zalmoxis** or **Zamolxes** = Dacians' main god, living on the tops of the Carpathian Mountains.

Grab sword and shield, disdaining vaunt!
We're born, and that's a cursed haunt:
But he who fears this battle now
Is free to leave before we vow,
And he who's here to scheme and taunt,
       Forsake us, anyhow!

There's not much more I need to say!
For now, your hands on shields you lay
The power of your hearts to show
And of the gods! Yet heroes, know:
The gods are yonder in the sky,
       But nearer is our foe!

george coşbuc

1866–1918

never has the autumn...

Never has the autumn seemed so fair and glowing
To our souls which, yearning towards death, will fade.
Silken rug the field is – pale, clear and flowing;
For the clouds, the trees are weaving their brocade.

Houses, like old pitchers, strung together, quiver
Fragrant wine spread cover thick inside their clay,
Lain in this blue haven of the sun-burned river,
From whose dirty mire, gold we drank all day.

Blackbirds in the sunset rise like sickly leaves
Of the hornbeam ancient, whiter in its hue.
Losing all its plumage, shaking as it gives
A farewell to the blue.

He who wants to weep, and he who wants to blame,
Come and hear the urging, strange and lonely gong.
And with eyes now glued on poplars' holy flame
Bury their own shadow, in their shadow's song.

1880-1967 tudor arghezi

testament

I won't leave much to you beyond my death,
A name inside a book perhaps, a breath,
In the rebellious evening, that ensues,
As my ancestors send to you their dues,
Through pits and furrows deep,
Scaled by my old folk in an angry creep,
That now await your youthful climb be done,
This book is but a simple step, my son.

Set it, in faith, as first and foremost guide,
And never put this holy writ aside,
For it belongs to slaves with loaded bales
Of ancient bones, through me becoming tales.

So that we're now translating, in a blink,
Spade into pen and furrow into ink,
My old folk gathered from amongst the snares,
Toil's perspiration for a hundred years.

1880-1967 tudor arghezi

And from their brogue, with prodding for the herd
Some fitting words I issued, undeterred,
Cribs for the masters' progeny to come.
And, kneaded for a thousand weeks till numb
I altered them in verse and icon true,
From rags, to flower buds and crowns for you.
The venom into honey to transform,
Preserving all its powers sweetly warm.
I took derision, spinning it demure,
And made it sometimes curse and sometimes lure.

The hearth, the dead ones' ashes, fire grown,
I took it and I made it God of stone;
A mighty border with two worlds in tow,
Guarding your duty's peak and all you know.

Our deaf and bitter pain, a deadly spin
I crammed it on a single violin,
That as he listened, promptly learned to dance
The master, like a slaughtered goat in trance.
From sores, and musty, muddy mold
I sprouted beauties, meanings new from old.

The suffered whip is turning into words
And slowly saves, with chastening from my scroll,
The living offspring from the crime of all.
The righteousness of an obscure old twig
Springing to light from forests dark and big
Blooming on top, a bunch of warts asunder,
The fruit of suffering, an ancient wonder.

Upon her couch, so lazily now lying,
The princess in my book is suffering, crying.
The writ of fire and the writ created,
Paired up, inside my book are married, mated.
Like grippers hugging iron, hot and strong
Writ by the slave, the master reads it wrong,
Suspecting not that deep within its pages
My forbears' wrath, silently rages.

1880-1967 tudor arghezi

psalm IV

I'm splitting you in noise and in calm
And stalking you as if you were some game,
To see: are you my hawk I wish to claim?
To kill you now? Or kneel to pray a psalm.

Be it in faith, be it in doubtful leap,
I seek you steadfast, yet without a goal.
You are my dream, your beauty I extol
And I don't dare to topple you from heaven in a heap.

Like mirrors on the water paths that fade
You now exist, you're gone now like a wish
I saw you in the stars, among the fish,
Like the wild bull, that's drinking in the shade.

In your grand story, we're a simple quiz,
To rate against you – that's why I remain,
Without intent the victory to gain.
I want to feel you and to scream: "He is!"

song IV
(to you the wind may pay a visit)

To you, the wind may pay a visit
And try to share my bitter story.
Don't let its wailing break your spirit,
And should it scold you, do not worry.

It's not your fault. It's just a habit
Of nature's law; I won't be crying.
The poisoned kiss of frost in autumn
Will touch a rose, she'll soon be dying.

But who will stop to sob in sorrow
When on the path a petal's wilting,
When all the forest's full of sunshine,
And full of joy the trees are tilting?

octavian goga

1881–1938

prayer

A wayward stray, with eyes a-mist,
My body wasted on this way,
I helplessly now fall, my master
And 'fore Your radiance I now lay.
My path is full of dark abysses
And darkness my horizon's holding,
I, on my knees, for You am seeking,
My Father, pray, my trail be molding!

Within my chest rocked by desires,
I feel temptations how they're linking,
They wish to turn to murky waters
The spring from which my soul is drinking.
From worldly waves tear me asunder,
And may Your counsel wisely sway;
On those I left behind forever,
Lord, make my gaze devoted stay.

Un-riddle for my mind the mystery,
The charms from nature's law above,
And in my arm forever settle
The strength of hate, the strength of love.
Grant me the song, grant me the light
Chime of a soul in love forever,
Grant summer sun rays in abundance
And my spent eyelids kindly lever.

octavian goga

1881–1938

Drive now away my deepest passions
Forever break their swaying power
And for the agony of others
Teach me to feel and weep each hour.
Not for my need forever pray.
Like some cruel fate, deceitful, evil,
But the dark sadness of the world,
May in my tears find its retrieval.

Grant me the bitterness and toil
Of many longings without cure,
Grant me a hurricane that's howling,
Where groans of slavery endure.
Since long ago have the downtrodden
Sighed with the world's weight on their shoulder...
Their frightening pain, my Lord, I'm begging,
Drop in my heart, make me its holder.

Sow in my soul the wildest tempest,
To feel how in its core, it struggles.
Taste bitterness that's overflowing,
And over quivering strings now juggles.
Let now beneath this burning vault
The lightning blue enamel gong,
Release its chiming voice of bronze,
And let our anguish sing its song.

ion minulescu

1881–1944

watercolor

In the city where it's raining for three days, each week unplanned
City people on the walkways,
Wander walking hand in hand.
In the city where it's raining for three days, each week unplanned,
From beneath the old umbrellas, which are sighing
And are bending,
Moist from raining without ending,
City people on the walkways
Look like automated puppets, fallen down from shop displays.

In the city where it's raining for three days each week unplanned
On the walkways there's no sound,
Save for footsteps of those found to be walking hand in hand,
Counting
In their minds

The rhythm of the chilly drops of rain,

From umbrellas, now descending,

From the drain pipes,

From the sky

With the power of a dye

Which endows a life that's slow,

Quite insipid,

Without purpose,

Without flow...

In the city where it's raining for three days, each week unplanned

An old couple looking bland –

Two old toys, so long now broken –

Wander, walking hand in hand...

romance without echo

Oh love, made of a porcelain so slim,
An object of ephemeral existence
I find you on the shelf, at the same distance
To where, last year,
I left you on a whim.

I'm thanking you!
But how did this occur?
What charitable soul helped you endure?
Without me here
And without her,
Without us both?
Which demon white,
Which bluebird swore the oath
To stay and watch for you so long
And take good care
So you don't break,
And you remain so fair?

Oh, love, made of a porcelain so slim,
A precious object with a glaze so pure,
Remain right here, your duty to fulfil;
Please do not move.
And if you love us still –
Oh! If you love us truly, love us deep –
Sing for another year the lover's hymn,
For just a year,
That's all,
Till we redeem
Our love made of a porcelain so slim!

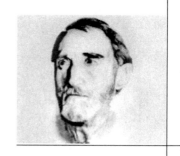

December

Behold how December is snowing…
Just gaze at the windows, my darling –
Command them to bring some more kindling
To hear the fire with its snarling.

My armchair, please shift near the wood stove,
A song will the storm now be humming,
Or maybe my days – same old goose chase –
Pray teach me their symphony drumming!

Command them to bring me the teapot,
Come closer, don't linger asunder –
Just read me a tale from the Arctic,
The snow will entomb us deep under.

1881–1957 george bacovia

How warm is your place, how becoming
And all in your house seems so holy –
Behold how December is snowing…
Don't laugh, read ahead for our folly.

The day is still lit, but what darkness…
Command them to bring me a lamp –
Behold, the snow's high like the fence now
And creeping up over the clamp.

I'm not going home for the evening
This deluge my nightmare is feeding,
Behold how December is snowing…
Don't laugh… remain calm, keep on reading.

1881–1957 george bacovia

lead

Entombed in sleep, the caskets made of lead
With leaden flowers and funerary cloak –
The crypt was windy... late when I awoke...
And creaking softly were the crowns of lead.

How deep my love was sleeping, turned, of lead
On leaden flowers, I called her sadly, shrill –
Alone near the corpse... I felt the chill...
And off its frame, were drooping wings of lead.

george bacovia

1881–1957

August

There are a few dead in town, my love
For this I came, I wished to let you know;
Up on the bier, from heat, inside the town
Cadavers fester silently and slow.

The living ones are moving, decomposed,
With clay for perspiration from the heat
Today it smells of cadavers, my love,
And now your breast is sagging just a bit.

Pour on the carpets strong perfumes and scents
Bring roses on your body to bestow;
There are a few dead in the town, my love,
Cadavers fester silently and slow...

1881–1957 george bacovia

fifty years

For fifty years, of stone made, and of clay
In every step, a start without delay.
And for the heat in which I'm anguished, pained
The holy unction from my forehead's drained.
Rise up, you, shady cedar and sit down
On afternoons of sweltering renown
With whisper pure, you throw across the deep
Your crown of night, and miracles to keep
Not for a rest. The opposite. For me,
I wish an angel as my enemy,
For you are weaker, worthless, never brave
The more your adversary is a knave.
I'd rather in your adumbration bustle,
To suck the force from him with whom I tussle.
My arm, rebellious, coils 'round him,
To feel the heaven's weight, filled to the brim.
For me, as if on purpose you allow,
To fight this planet's refuse until now.
Though there's this sign that I forever try
To be disciple of the fights on high:
I've fifty stone-slabs, glowing without falter,
Completing to your glory holy altar.

vasile voiculescu

1884–1963

song for undressing

How many silken angels watch you play?
In tender cloud, when flying they escape,
Revealed are breasts and arms, ray after ray,
Out from the treasures of your graceful shape.

Smooth star lights are your reconciling thighs
Round laws they promulgate as you lay down;
From flesh and from eternity you rise
And wear delicious truths – a lovely gown.

Unbuttoning a star, the clouds release
Your waist, like heaven's vault, deep and replete,
Your legs, which long, like milky ways, decrease
Fortunes of thin ankles, dainty feet.

Your shadow, pure and white, appears to me
Like angels and like clouds – you naked soar
Long will my kisses raise in earnest plea,
The truth of your sweet figure to explore.

the last pretend sonnets of Shakespeare in an imaginary translation by V. Voiculescu – CLXXXII

I've not been an apprentice, anyway;
But from the start, accomplished artist... still
Unequalled master, before you, I pray,
Pour now your grace upon me, if you will.
Don't think it strange: I beg don't judge my size,
Lend me instead your all; you can't divide
Your Love from its great sisters; may your eyes
On Timeless Art and sovereign Death abide...
Today, quite happy, they no more meander
Disintegrated, through this world, and lost:
From hell, from heaven, and from earth asunder,
Into your dazzling beauty, they are tossed.
      Hence, when my head onto your breast I place
      All three of them together I embrace.

1884–1963   vasile voiculescu

October

george topîrceanu

1886 - 1937

October left upon the hills
 A tapestry of red and yellow.
The silver clouds are wavy quills
        Sad love songs cry the rooster's bellow.

I grip on the barometer
And shudder if it drops a pin
The sun is getting smaller in
        Diameter.

But from warm heavens, like in May
Days follow after pale days,
They are more fickle and less gay
        In subtle ways...

And turning late, at her own leisure
The Autumn walks through gardens, bowers,
Her gown folds filled in hefty measure
        With ruffled flowers.

Her glide, designed to overwhelm
And to despise,
Precisely so that the whole realm
        Stares after her in stark surprise,

A lilac, haplessly would glower
At her allurement so sublime
And turning yellow for an hour
In his excitement went to flower

        A second time...

the ant

At golden calm of evening, unruffled, the man hoes...
The heavy plough, the oxen, and he, all look like pawns
Of wood on chessboards black and green across the lawns:
Above them reigns majestic, a sky in spring repose.

In furrows turned forever, in germinating soil
Unleavened bread, pale offerings – for other children meant,
He deeply sinks the iron, his thoughts all grey and bent
He stops, his body broken by centuries of toil.

He doesn't see beside him, his comrade, busy, scant,
On grass, dragging her sorrow – so heavy walks the ant,
Who also didn't notice the giant, wasn't awed.

And now when night erases all: ant, man, and skyline bright,
Not one of them is sensing the heavens where lives God
Who ploughs, as blind as they are, the vast and starry height.

ion pillat

1891–1945

King Crypto and the Lapp Enigel

ion barbu

1895-1961

Oh minstrel sad, obscurer, still,
Than good old wine they serve at weddings
Which the groom's father dished at will
With bags and ribbons, tinsel meldings,

Most stubborn minstrel might as well
That grand old song to try and sing,
Tell of the small Lapp Enigel,
And good old Crypto, mushroom-king!

Chief here's my grief!
Your feast, my tongue did burn and sting,
I'll sing that song, although not brief,
Of Enigel and Crypto king.

Sing minstrel, sing!
You sang last summer like a heller;
Now sing constrained, on a quiet string,
To end the wedding in the cellar.

*

Oft searched by forests' wild young sons
In river bed and greasy clay,
Reigned over mushrooms' fleshy buns
King Crypto's heart of dark dismay,

On some eternal dewy throne!
The mushrooms prattled on, however,
That Penny Bun, the witch, did hone
A brew to keep him young forever.

And hateful snowdrops tall or stumpy
From dampest pits were crying sour,
Conjectured he'd be fruitless, jumpy
Because he didn't want to flower.

In lands of ice forever doomed,
In those same days, down some deep dell,
A small and quiet girl was groomed,
The Lapp with furs named – Enigel.

From winter dream to grazing stream,
To a new year, her reindeer bade,
Through dew, she ran, towards the sun,
On moss she lay, her running done,
Near Crypto, young groom of the glade.

Three rugs she made, beneath the shade
Gently she slept, dreaming sweet cherries,
When at her chest, bald king would rest,
Who dragged his eunuch on this quest,
Luring with nectar like the fairies:

1895–1961 ion barbu

– Enigel, Enigel,
I have brought you jam, look here.
Berries too, just for you
Take some, eat them, have no fear.

– Bald king pressed near my chest,
Thank you for your grace and skill.
But I wish to collect
My fresh berries down the hill.

– Enigel, Enigel,
Night is ebbing, light is lifting,
If you go to collect,
Start with me, don't go a-drifting.

– I would pick you, kind bald king...
But the dawn has started dancing
And you're dainty, frail with sap:
I do fear that soon you'll snap,
Ripen first, then come romancing.

– Me to ripen, Enigel,
How I'd wish, but from the sun,
A hundred nightmares, burning hell,
Cut me off. He's red, no fun,
Should I stay, it's my death knell;
Please forget him Enigel,
My cool shadow do not shun.

– Crypto king, Crypto king,
Like a blasted sword-edge sheer
In my heart, these words do sting!
For the dark, I greatly fear,

Because in winter I'm conceived,
And cousin with the arctic bear,
From the dark shadow now retrieved,
The sun I worship, wise and fair.

With lamps of ice and under snows
My whole north pole one dream is dreaming.
Green-tinged, a platter grand which grows
Of purest gold, our fancy gleaming.

The sun I worship, old and wise,
My soul's a fountain, on the rise,
The big white wheel, he is my master,
Deep in my soul, a holy aster.

When sunny, does the wheel grow large;
But shadows put the flesh in charge;
Asleep's the flesh, and weak as gel,
But wind and shadows make it swell...

1895–1961 ion barbu

Pleasingly spoke, with dainty knell,
The small straightforward, Enigel,
But time, you see, was waiting not,
And the big sun rose like a shot,
Up in the skies, a ring of hell.

– Oh cry, you sweet, wise Enigel!
For how could Crypto, mushroom chief,
Love that hot light, which brought him grief?
He peels off lightly, like a shell,
From Enigel,
In the soft shadow to find fief...

But the hot sun, that fiery king,
Mirrored in him his deadly ring;
Ten times it did it, without shame
On his bald skin mirrored a flame;

And his sweet sap is getting sour!
His hidden heart will burst this hour,
Into ten darkened seals alive;
Red venom from a deadly hive
Seeping deep curses, now arrive;

It's tough, the sun for long to bear,
For frail wood mushrooms in the glare,
Because their souls are kept cool,
Unlike for man, old beastly fool;
But to a creature, dainty, frail,
That whimsy is a poisoned grail.

– Like crazy Crypto, of love spurned,
Whose heart in him the fire burned,
And he was left to wander on
With a more princely face of scorn:

With Dragon Mute, that grand old brute,
To cast the world some gold for loot,
To chop it, naked he will flee,
For it is Penny Bun, you see,
Whom he has asked his queen to be.

ion barbu

1895-1961

lucian blaga

1895-1961

I do not crush the crown of this world's wonders

I do not crush the crown of this world's wonders,
and do not kill
with my mind the mysteries which I encounter
on my way
in flowers, in eyes, on lips or just on tombstones.
Others' bright light
extinguishes the spell of the obscure,
the enigmatic, hidden in the depths of darkness,
but I,
I with my light augment the world's enigma –
just like the moon, with its white ray
which won't diminish, but quivering
increases the night's puzzle,
in the same way do I enrich the shadows of horizons
with wondrous awe of holy riddles
and all that's undiscerned
transforms itself in even larger un-discernments
under my gaze –
for I'm in love
with flowers, and eyes, and lips, and all the tombstones.

to waste is prone the month of May

This simple, undisguised occurrence,
too late, some day, we might remember,
the garden bench on which we rested,
our temples touching, crimson ember.

Hazelnut trees are raining cinders,
white poplars join a wild array.
To be profuse craves each new dawn,
to waste is prone the month of May.

Sweet pollen falls on us again,
like yellow snowdrifts, gentle cover,
as if some fine and golden threads.
Shoulders and eyelashes discover.

lucian blaga

1895-1961

For our mouths will taste it speaking,
while in our eyes the word goes missing.
We can't predict regretful evenings,
as we lay sleepless, reminiscing.

This simple, undisguised, occurrence,
too late, some day, we might remember,
the garden bench on which we rested,
our temples touching, crimson ember.

Through dreams and longings now we linger –
this gold dust hides a bitter twist –
lush forests latently existing
forever failing to exist.

1895–1961 lucian blaga

Eve

When the serpent gave Eve the fruit, he spoke to her
with a bellowing voice
chiming among the leaves, like a silver bell.
But it so happened that later he whispered
something in her ear,
softly, very softly
something which is not written in the scriptures.

Not even God heard exactly what he whispered to her,
even though
He was trying to listen too.
And Eve didn't want to tell
Adam either.

Ever since, the woman hides a secret underneath her eyelids
and moves her eyelashes as if to say
that she knows something
which we don't,
and no one does,
not even God.

1895–1961 lucian blaga

ion vinea

1895-1964

to the one who came

May your hands be, for me, the last
to lay down for the heart
the snow of the primordial silence
as if over a new tomb of autumn.

May your eyes be the somber sun
of the world of sleep
towards which my soul gets resurrected.

May your voice be for me the gentle breeze
of the far away seas in which the heavy bells
of prayer grew faint.

May your hair tresses be for me
the evening weeping willow
in which the whispers tremble, forgotten.

May your soul be for me a kiss
on cold eyelids
and your tear
the clear conscience of the last moment.

May the late love
be the wave binding us
to eternity.

revolt

I dream of a revolt of the vegetation realm.

From the pale lichen living beyond the polar regions
To arbors from the tropics, so huge! – they overwhelm,
With mushrooms, flowers, shoots, the cedar and the elm,
They rise against the human usurpers in their legions,
Restoring their primeval control over the realm.

The migrant bird
Has carried over every continent
The marvelous word;
And now in every shoot and flower gird
The demon of revolt grows subtle, violent.

The eucalypts and pines with giant arms
Bubonic old boabs, with bulges on their trunks
Are marching, ghastly, on the cities, in their swarms
And crushing bridges, palaces, and towers into dust.

From equator's deep burrows
Young vines with snaky arms like hydras and like dragons
Invisible they creep
To gain their burst
And in a web of living ropes, they sweep
This earth that's cursed.

alexandru philippide

1900–1979

And nameless trees, with huge harpoon-like arms,
Grow dreadful from the jungle, like hurricanes they blow,
And march out from the darkness with boa snakes in tow,
While screaming monkeys trumpet their loud and fierce alarms.

A copse of large sequoias is starting its assault,
It covers a huge distance in just a single vault
And with a gale, reaches its goal:
You watch how a sky-scraper of glass and steel, will roll
And crash inertly to a halt,
Colossal stupid troll.

From the taiga armies of pines rush out,
With huge strides from their roots they move about
Like ugly gnarled phalanges;
They are so thick together, that they stop
All large monsoon-like rivers with their mop –
A small, dry, creek has now become the Ganges.

From tree branches, as though from slingshots high,
Enormous rocks are shooting, as if from distant stars;
They fall upon the earth in huge array
And fill the oceans like some deadly scars.

In every blade of grass, there grows a thorn,
In every leaf, a hidden eye will throb;
And in the ground, in tubes and bulbs is born
A dark malignant broth – which many lives will rob.

A force which has been stifled for twenty thousand years
Stayed hidden in the stillness of sap and wind and earth
And now with groaning earthquakes and with volcano sneers
The vegetation era is ushered like a birth…

… To last so long until perhaps, one day
In eons of the future, a time so far away,
The metals in the darkness and rocks which, dormant, prey,
Good sisters with the stars – a burning hell -
They will awake from stagnant nights as well.

whispered song

Some time ago I killed a sparrow,
I slung a stone and her life I robbed.
And then the whole day and the night that followed,
I mourned for her and for her I sobbed.

Mother did not punish me, she did not chide,
In my hand, I was holding a piece of bread.
"It is in vain", she said, "in vain you are weeping,
What has died will remain with the dead."

Later on, when I was a young lad
I fell madly in love, a fair girl I embraced.
I don't know why, but one day she died
And another day, she was laid to rest.

It is long since I slung a stone at a sparrow,
It's long since funerals have frightened me.
The sun is setting there beyond some hills
And it rises in flames from the sea.

I stopped aiming stones at storks and at sparrows
I stopped firing my gun at the deer.
And this is, perhaps, the reason my song
Remains young, remains fresh, every year.

This song of mine is a whispered song,
All my songs tell a whispered story,
Some are meant for your lovely ears, while others
For the ears of this world full of glory.

1902-1974 zaharia stancu

rise up now Gheorghe, rise up now Ion!

Not for a shovel of ruddy hot bread,
not for barns full of grain, nor for fields full of corn,
but for a tomorrow with your sky free of dread,
rise up now Gheorghe, rise up now Ion!

For the blood of your folk flowing red through the drains,
for your beautiful song which was stifled at morn,
for the tears of your sun, left imprisoned in chains,
rise up now Gheorghe, rise up now Ion!

Not for your fury sinking teeth into bars,
but to sing as you fill, on the crest of the dawn,
a heap of horizons and a hatful of stars,
rise up now Gheorghe, rise up now Ion!

So that freedom you drink, flowing fresh from the pail,
and to heavenly whirlpools be mightily drawn,
while apricot flowers drop on you, merry hail,
rise up now Gheorghe, rise up now Ion!

And so, as you kindle your kisses on fires,
on thresholds and doors, which the icons adorn,
on all that is free and for freedom desires,
rise up now Gheorghe, rise up now Ion!

Rise up now Gheorghe on chains and on ropes!
Rise up now Ion on the heavenly bone!
And high, to the storm-light which shines on your hopes,
rise up now Gheorghe, rise up now Ion!

1905-1975 radu gyr

late last night, Jesus...

Late last night Jesus came and He entered my cell.
Oh, how sad and how lofty seemed Christ!
The moon, which followed Him into the cell,
made taller and sadder, the Sacrificed.

His hands looked like lilies on gloomy tombstones,
His eyes, dark like the sunless woodlands.
The moon on His garment shone silvery tones
and silver-like scars on His hands.

Amazed, I jumped from under my sheet
– From whence come you, Lord, from what time?
He touched His lips with a finger, discrete
to be silent, to me He did mime…

He sat down with me on the carpet dust:
– On My wounds put your hand, feel the scars!
His ankles bore shadows of wounds and of rust
as if from dragging shackles and bars…

He sighed as He rested His weary, beat, bones
on my rug full of vermin, foul, black.
The moonlight was throwing long, sinister tones
like rods on the snow of His back.

The cell seemed a mountain, a forehead so grand,
tribes of lice and of rats ruled this field.
I felt how my heavy head fell on my hand
to a thousand years' sleep, I was wheeled.

Later, when I awoke, the queer darkness was gone,
and the hay was fragrant like roses and light.
The moon shone in my cell, but I was alone
for Jesus was nowhere in sight...

I stretched my arms wide. No one here, so hushed.
I queried the wall. No reply!
Only razor cold rays from dark corners,
they rushed and their lance pierced my side in their fly.

– Where are you, Lord? – I screamed at the grate.
A smoke, as of incense, the moon now trails.
I touched my body, and my hands, oh what fate!
carried the deep scars of His nails.

1905-1975 radu gyr

the last letter

The ending has arrived without a warning.

You're happy now? I see you wear a ring.

I understand and sever without mourning

The useless hope. You follow the same thing!

No, not a word. Don't say it's just a form,

 I understand full well the hidden sense.

I know, you have in life a different norm,

But I don't worship norms, there's no pretense.

I'll no more sing, will never more exult,

And neither will I cross your path again,

I do not blame you, it is not your fault.

What more to say? It's needless to explain.

Mistaken though it was, that is for sure

It could have been amazing, it was naught.

And in my boredom, everlasting, pure

I still won't know if you could give a thought.

And still, and still, there was a touch or two

Enough to make me stagger on the way

The open heavens with an angel's hue

Threw light onto my evenings' dismay.

When Midas' fingers I have put to magic

Caress your tender being made of clay

It rang in me a watery, pelagic,

Sound of creation from the primal day.

1907-1988   mihai beniuc

I saw how, over eons, was ascending

Your golden statue, luminous and heavy

And how the centuries, quietly attending

In muted rows would kneel and pay your levy,

While at your pedestal, without a motion

They'd wait for you to open, full of grace,

Your holy hand, to kiss in pure devotion

Before they disappear without a trace.

Oh, if we were together but one hour,

We would have lived a golden dream, unbroken,

Like an eternal and resplendent flower,

Which can't be known, and can't be spoken.

Predestined came the ending to our tale,

And I don't know if you indeed will stare

By chance upon this letter – for I fail

To sway you to remain the way you were.

I shall not squash the dream, or speak in jest;

I shall not stain with words what I hold dear.

I could have said: "You are like all the rest..."

But I refuse to sully and to sneer.

For even though you'd swim in ugly mire,

You shall remain as waterlily's snow

Which mirrored in a lake of drunk desire,

Reflects you pure from memories aglow.

mihai beniuc

1907–1988

101

Forever I'll believe, I'll never doubt,
Without a word my love will press along,
Meanwhile, the world will never figure out
Why other women never hear my song.
For there, under the magic rays of yore,
Cleansed in the quiet waters of my dream,
Adored you'll linger, in the sky to soar,
An evening star so kind and so serene.
And should this life be rough and cruel, you see,
When people will throw mud and stones at you,
Be sure to run into a dream to me,
The two of us in harmony anew.
My tears will wash away your every stain,
Unwritten verses will caress you sweet.
And in their swaying rhythm, they'll refrain
Your early dream of happiness replete.
And if it happens (as I feel of late)
For me to have to leave and wave goodbye,
If I should hear your calling at the gate,
The frosty grave will hear my awful cry.
But if I cannot hope to cross again,
If those dark borders be forever sealed,
I'd struggle wretched in that wintry reign,
And howl into the gloom, and never yield.

marine

In your eyes, like in mirrors, twilight oceans are drifting
From the sea, drops of sun burning bright, wanton spree;
Oh, but little remains, and the magic is lifting...
It's too little, you see,
It's too little, you see.

Sip the ring of the sky, make it white alabaster!
Draw the sea in your lungs, sighed abyss like a plea!
Let the wind moan away in our heart, wilting aster...
It's so little, you see,
It's so little, you see.

Tell me why should we trample our joy to the ground?
As the sky speaks of fire, horrors burn our endeavor;
And for all that we love, death is lurching around...
It's been lurching forever.
We've rebuffed it forever.

For this moment I pray, just the moment that's fleeting,
– When my soul longs in bitter and fearsome reprieve –
Just your smile will abide, and beholding your greeting...
It's too much to conceive,
It's too much to conceive.

Bring your bright star along, make it ripe like a cherry,
Let me bite, let me breathe, let me feel you and hear;
For the seconds are burning and the evening is eerie...
It's too little I fear,
And it's plenty I fear.

cicerone theodorescu

1908–1974

the pale horse

That pale horse, that pale horse
With saddle blue,
Keep it, my Lord, keep it, my Lord,
I'm begging you!...

Long time ago there was a creature
Like a chess tower with no feature
Which got involved with a pale horse
For wine is sweet each year, of course.

REFRAIN
That pale horse, that pale horse
The wine will flow,
I'd stay, of course, I'd stay, of course
And wouldn't go!

Out of the blue as if by chance
An officer appeared in style
With clicking spurs as in a dance
(His iron heels would walk a mile).

And when, one day, my pale horse
Was trotting gently on the lawn
That officer, without recourse,
Swept it aside like some poor pawn.

The tower, sadly, died from weeping,
As cruel, the enemies were creeping
As for the king, he died conceited
But wouldn't give himself defeated.

spectacle

The elite took their seats on the first level
and the idiots, high up, close to heaven.
In the box, an occurrence with a broken heart
near a cruel destiny dressed up very smart.
A disaster, so strong, you couldn't sway,
was hoping it would all blow away.
A shipwreck was dozing in the armchair -
rugged up in a shroud, dark with despair.
A simple cold
Was traipsing the hall, getting old.
An innocence
was shining by leaving us in total suspense.
The play was a brawl
between virtue and fall.
The scene was an altar on holy ground
in which the truth only seldom was found.
The actors would mumble their role
but the mud would swallow them whole.
In the pauses, silent applauses
At the end of the game, silent acclaim.
And when the curtain fell,
all wondered who would go to hell
and who's the author of the rhyme
who committed this crime

1911–1977 emil botta

in five acts, full of verve
like a murder with nerve.
But then Ariel came into the limelight
with garlands of flames and of anemone
to gift the "dramatis personae" honourably.
And this fiction etched in ink with some friction
took the droll spectacle close to eviction
to oblivion and dereliction.

talion

An eye for a nose tooth for a flower
horse for blood man for fruit
then there is that uninterrupted house
and that felt knife made of water
there were many drawers made of fog
there was a chair becoming a virtue
and then there were those letterboxes full of leaves
 and feet and boots and melancholy
and a few words in a wooden tube
and I don't know where and I don't know why

and all were compensating and compensating

gifts

You are for me a precious, cherished gift
so unexpected, full of sweet surprise.
I search for you again and often drift
to dream, for my delight I can't disguise.

You are my secret strength and cryptic pride,
and since I've known you, heavens bear no toll,
in vain the pains and sufferings abide,
to adumbrate the waters of my soul.

My body's dust is lighter now, unsealed;
my heart is resting heavy, walled with love,
like fruitful branches, which in autumn yield,
and blessings carry, as you look above.

Gigantic, like the sky, replete with stars,
my soul's reflecting you as in a lake,
and deep, since then, my thoughts, like wealthy czars,
regard the dust of heartache, meager, fake.

And if I were to pay you for all these,
I couldn't, so my prodigal, don't spurn
the truth that I do love you, for, with ease,
the gifts you gave, I'll gift you in return.

magda isanos

1916–1944

I carry you within

I carry you within, a precious vessel,

A hidden treasure in my heart will nestle,

In my own body, white and heavy breast,

Like pomegranate's seed in fruit does rest.

I hold you in my mind, a holy tune,

An ancient song, an Eastern prince to swoon.

Around my neck, I wear this priceless lace,

Your arm is holding mine, a shroud of grace.

I carry you within, a secret dream,

In lofty night skies, I entwined your beam.

I carry you, the rosy morning light,

Like flowers' scent, so fresh and clear and bright.

A honeycomb I carry on my lips,

A golden fig, which heaven's nectar drips.

I carry you within my arms, fine quilt,

A carefully laid cluster threaded gilt.

Like apricots in flower, their fruit yielding,

In daydream bright, you, deep within I'm shielding.

zorica laţcu

1917-1990

motherland

I behold you with the reversed spyglass
Of my heart, as if from on top of a hillock.
No matter how far, no matter how much,
Through the Monday of a moment, my country,
I salute you.

I have not forgotten the smell of the gentle orchards
And even the scattered smell of the big city,
That too I have not forgotten, and sometimes
In a dream, a street sneezes in me
As it crosses another.

And still I see it, as if it was today, before me,
The moon counting the branches of elms,
On the long provincial boulevards,
Alongside the tired Danube,
Tying a ribbon on the hip of my country.

Through these worlds, sometimes transfixed,
The evening rises in me, like a wind,
All the leaves of the great village-fair,
All the cries of the barefoot Oltenians*,
From a district to another.

---

* **Olteni** – people from the region of Oltenia, in southern Romania.

ştefan baciu

1918–1993

I preserve you within my soul, my sad country,
Fertile soil, suffering from hunger,
And I cannot forget, not even in my sleep,
That in the bitter days you fed
My longing for freedom.

It's only in the evenings that you seem pure to me,
Among all the cold stars, a warm one,
And in the night, as black as your vast sea,
I sleep with you under my pillow erecting
Your ineffable face in an immaculate tear.

adolescence

Wind and groves, and eighteen years of age…
Street with chestnut trees and fragrant sage,
springtime on the resurrected lake
days, which kissed by memories, awake…

Girl with waist as of a violin,
where did our Latin book begin?
ablatives mixed in, scribbled and lost,
with the halting couplet that we tossed?
In your deep blue eyes, you were collecting
untranslated poems, unsuspecting,
and your gentle deer-like walk, in prayer,
scribed calligraphy of rhyme, so rare...

While the Danube aired the stars on high,
we would count them in the evening sky,
water lilies from the moon would sever,
as we learned the lovers' word, forever.
Through cathedrals, arching willows weeping,
our small boat was gliding, slowly creeping
to a land of silences and reed.
Thoughts, like seagulls, to the heaven heed.
Our kiss surges high and sails pure
tasting like the berries of the moor,

mihu dragomir

1919–1964

sweet and bitter, dark and crimson leap,
anaphora rising from the deep.
On the sand of golden beaches laid,
laurel crowns the sun for us has made,
my sweet girl, of Danube and of hushes,
my sweet girl, with hair like midnight blushes...

Dreamlike groves, with chestnut trees and sage,
wind and sand, and eighteen years of age...

corydon

I am the most handsome of all in this town,
The crammed streets are stunned as I walk without peer
So sparkling and graceful the ring in my ear
And so full of flowers my tie and my gown.
I am the most handsome of all in this town.

Conceived by the incest of sun rays and twilight
My gaze, with its splendor, caresses the dark,
The whole town is abuzz about me and my mark,
They fear me in secret, though, still, I'm their highlight.
I'm the Prince of penumbrae, I am lord of half-light…

I cannot avoid their lascivious gaze,
It waves through my hair like a silvery thread,
And all of them ask: am I living, or dead?
Why wear bright green socks, or a pasha's red fez?
There is no escape, though I'd hide in a maze…

My body with ribbons and sashes I cover,
The earth is a pedestal, high for my stride.
One pink eye remains under eyeglass to hide,
And then my whole leg, when I step, I uncover,
But quickly I cover it, once again to uncover…

1920-1962 radu stanca

The other eye (yellow one) I let it watch
The people who hold me as if clutching their dream.
Ha! Ha! If you knew just how silly you seem,
As you jump and you hop, for my black lips to touch.
The other eye watches, and I let it watch.

A secret face-pencil enhances my form
I bathe in fresh cider three times every night,
No spittle but milk drool my lips, creamy-white,
Monk shoes help my slenderness step through the storm,
My virtue's enhanced through pig's blood, thick and warm.

All the teeth in my mouth are plated with gold,
My waist is well tucked into a corset and shirt,
I smoke a huge opium pipe with a squirt,
On my arm's a tattoo, of a bull big and bold,
And the jewels on my crown are a sight to behold!

Through my long and mysterious nails – what fright! –
The hideous cat-head umbrella is grinning,
And I don't know why, when I'm happy and winning,
As I lead all the people to temptation and sinning,
From me jump some snakes full of poison and bite,

1920-1962 radu stanca

Like trees, I sprout branches and twigs silky, light,
And nature itself, omniscient with reason,
Is unsure what I am: man or flower, or season,
A tower perhaps, setting houses alight,
A tower with gems falling down, precious, bright.

I am the most handsome of all in this town,
The crammed streets are stunned as I walk without peer,
So sparkling and graceful the ring in my ear,
And so full of flowers my tie and my gown.
I am the most handsome of all in this town.

1920–1962 radu stanca

the silver-fanged boar

ştefan augustin doinaş

1922-2002

A Levantine prince quite enamored with hunting,
some dark-hearted forest was travelling through
and making his path with great effort and grunting,
he said, while on bone-flute he merrily blew:

– Let's hunt through these forests, untrodden and daunting,
the silver-fanged boar who's ferocious and wild,
who changes his fur every day, as he's molting,
and changes his hooves, and his glass eye reviled....

– Oh, master, the servants with trumpets would say,
that bloodthirsty boar does not travel through here.
It's better to chase down the antlers to slay,
or red colored foxes, or hares that are near....

But smiling and certain the prince passed ahead
and carefully gazing at trees and their hues,
he left in his lair the young deer full of dread,
and the sparkly eyed lynx who'll smile for a ruse.

Through beech woods he'd trample old weeds to the ground:
– Just look how he turns! We have closed in for good
on this silver-fanged boar, not too far, hear his sound:
come over, let's hit him with arrows of wood!...

– My lord, it's the stream through the woods, tall and lush,
the smart servant said, as he laughed with a roar.
But the prince turned around and replied only: – Hush...
And the water did shine like the fang of a boar.

Under elm trees he'd hasten his scattered old train:
– You see how he's puffing alone and unreal,
the silver-fanged boar over meadow and plain:
come over, let's hit him with arrows of steel!

– My lord, it's the grass that with boots we would brush,
the bold-looking servant would say like before.
But the prince turned around to reply only: – Hush...
And the glistening grass seemed like fangs of a boar.

Under firs, he would cry pushing them to the peak:
– You see where he's finding his lair and his shire,
the boar from old tales, of whom old people speak:
– come over, let's hit him with arrows of fire!…

– My lord, it's the moonlight which night fears can't quash,
the servant said laughing, despising and sore.
But turning around the prince only said: – Hush...
And the moonlight shone bright, like the fangs of a boar.

ştefan augustin doinaş

1922-2002

Alas! under rays of the pale stars at dusk,
as he crouched for a drink, his knees slowly sagged,
there charged a huge boar with his piercing sharp tusk
and the prince through the red dust he savagely dragged.

– What strange looking beast so bloodthirsty and vicious,
is stopping the hunt for my silver-fanged boar?
What black bird is crying in moonlight so listless?What
wilted old leaf shakes my soul to its core?...

– My master, that boar with the fangs as of silver,
that same had you pierced, and with blood you're awash.
The dogs chase it now - can't you hear? by the river... But
turning, the prince whispered quietly: – Hush.

You take the old horn, and just blow without pause
to sound till I'm dead, to the sky clear and prime...
Right then from the ridges a big moon arose,
and the horn made its sound for a very short time.

epitaph

From all we've said, and all we hail,
remains a tear, bewildered, shy
an ancient poem, lonely tale,
which of itself will fade and die

the same as other poems faded
and trailing us, or trailing it,
the maples rest on evenings, jaded,
through someone's eyes, now dimly lit

like in a water glass in which
the well itself is crawling flat
its coolness dying in some ditch
or hardly that... or hardly that...

ion caraion

1923-1986

execution

federico garcia lorca
       was shattering
– under the spray of bullets! –
    on the road to cordoba!

one after another
     they died
  villon, edgar poe, verlaine

the fourth time
     he did not get himself up anymore
       he no longer wanted to!

… ay,
they started shooting
  also
    in the poets
      not yet born!!

1923-1983 darie magheru

the little prince

eulogy to innocence

I know to enquire
of a lamb or a mountain.
And once in a forest
I kissed a small fountain.

I know how surprised
is the color blue.
I have a garden
and a window view.

I also have a book
very thin and small,
which only has space
for one love to scrawl.

Can I take my place,
near you, on the star?
– Sure, replied the prince.
You're my friend from afar.

1924 – 2014 nina cassian

destiny with a boab

leonid dimov

1926–1987

The city danced a paperboard quadrille
In cinemas; and scared, against their will,
The streets would lift hushed burdens up to heaven,
But just between the brakes. At five and seven.
The square, which famous Swabians would swab
Lay dwarfed beneath a towering boab
Its forehead like a house, and with a pub,
With pearly trains at speed through bough and shrub.
With blue stops, where we'd smile and drink away
From lucent absinthe glasses through the day,
And laughing, we'd tell stories and we'd pass
Dumb comments to the fish behind the glass,
That evening when a still and tender cloud
Mirrored a rooster and a barking sound,
The Swabian doctors lovingly would swab
Sick patients hanging in the huge boab.

escape

I need to run
from the table
on which I cut
this slice of bread
because the table and the bread

and the knife
are a kingdom
teaching me

that I am here
and that I am doing too well

delectatio morosa

how perverse are oh Lord
the pleasures of old age
why would I ever want
to be young again?

irina mavrodin

1929-2012

ending

To write the hundredth sonnet. On the way

This boundary stone, this bollard standing guard,
I hate all endings, I would have them barred
Today I won't delay. "For here I stay".
Like on a war field. Some alive, some dead;
Raptured to heaven, or just resurrected.
Like in a dream a Judgment full of dread.
You find by asking; climbing you're rejected.
Or it is Noah with his ark who wouldn't bar
You from the bridge – you're in your prime.
A road, pray tell, like centuries of years!
You can't see clouds. A sign I draw with tears
Alone. On the horizon the same star.

All other signs, through boundless time.

1930 – aurel rău

reading the coffee dregs

my lord
one can no more compete today
the Japanese cup lays in a shattered state
 and black, the coffee dregs seem to convey
a vicious dog appearing at the gate

the musketeers you hope that soon you'll see
three foils in their buttonhole polite
to tell you that a new poète maudit*
using a garter, hanged himself last night

the error's in the cardinal mauve bright
who saw sweet lorelei disguised and scheming
as fishermen were drunk and sleeping tight
while of some tigris and euphrates dreaming

you are condemned, my lord, to cultivate
for each and every day a pink carnation
in vestal paradises, snakes mutate,
beneath your sole, your own deification

what more a king could dream for, what indeed,
as quaint, the window's triangle grows blue
my lord
one can no more compete today
take off and hang your coat, for that will do

---

* A **poète maudit** (from French, *accursed poet*) lives a life outside or against society,
abuses drugs and alcohol, is prone to insanity, often resulting in an early death.

1931 – nora iuga

myopia

in the evening, she tells me – today suzana herself read in my coffee,

describing how a man with round googly eyes,

was running chasing after me – does that mean

that it is some man wearing glasses? (I quickly take

my lenses off my nose and blow on them

to chase away temptations) but later on –

suzana was saying (she continues),

that suddenly there's a street corner and you escape – this is exactly

what I am fearing, she added thoughtfully. seen without glasses,

her face is like some opinion – I'm thinking of what I wrote long ago

that my links to time are like the run

of an insane man who wants to catch up

with himself – and there is always a corner.

in the end, I put my glasses on and everything returns back to normal.

1931–2011 mircea ivănescu

registers

My birth is recorded in the register
my baptism is calligraphed into the register too
the diagram of my diligence and of my laziness –
followed up through mountains of school registers
once upon a time stealing a rose, to give it to you,
I was punished and recorded in the register
between some pages with coarse headings
sits, sealed meekly,
my eternal love for you
our son: recorded in the register too
over and over again Petre Stoica present in the registers:
for illnesses for thoughts for so many debts
not repaid on time
until the day the lid on the coffin of the thick register
will fall for the last time
on my name,
the name of a man who's left the world of the living

twenty-one dreams

1.

I dreamed that I was sleeping in the bed of a sweet queen

2.

I dreamed that I was throwing one million dollars out the window

3.

I dreamed that I knew how to resolve subtle mathematical problems

4.

I dreamed that I was smacking the bottoms of the children of an obese dictator

5.

I dreamed that my eagle was tearing the stripes off the trousers of warring generals

6.

I dreamed that I was shooting my pistol into the dark heart of the world

7.

I dreamed that I gave a poisoned flower to an executioner who happened to know me

8.

I dreamed that I was playing nine men's morris with the chamberlain of an emperor from the last century

9.

I dreamed that I was marrying the daughter of a grocer who still had a memory of the husks

10.

I dreamed that my alter-ego was strolling in the shade wearing sunglasses

petre stoica

1931–2009

11.

I dreamed that I was in the presence of a pendulum clock which ground
everything

12.

I dreamed that I was wearing pants made of flour a shirt made of water and a
hat made of fire

13.

I dreamed that I was dancing on the beach with a lit candle on my head

14.

I dreamed that I was majestically stepping out of a mirror framed with
stinging nettles

15.

I dreamed that I was gifting myself a big bunch of lovage for my birthday

16.

I dreamed that I was directing city traffic in the opposite direction

17.

I dreamed that I was being accepted just as I am in reality

18.

I dreamed that I hiccupped and sneezed in an ideal manner

19.

I dreamed that I was being exhibited in a coffin with lilac wings

20.

I dreamed that I was finding relief from a millennial toothache

21.

at the same time, I dreamed that I had the most elastic straps in the whole
world

daily journal

We are all running seeking that unique way
which every one of us must find by ourselves.

Pray, tell me, what cosmic speed have we reached now?

Rain surrounds some of us with bars
as if we were in some kind of birdcage.
Others deal in hope, which they sell
illegally
at the highways and by the hedges.
While others play guardians by the doors of some
empty houses.
Still others...

The sea, because it does not know how to do anything,
mills without ceasing some images encountered on the way
hitting them continuously against one another.

moon in the field

With my left hand, I turned your face towards me,
beneath the tent of the sleepy quince tree,
and if my gaze could leave your eyes and wander,
the sweep of even sky would velvet be.

I would imagine fathoming through branches,
strong hunters chasing lions in their might,
on horseback pulling strings of bows and arrows.
Oh, stretch your left hand, let them go tonight

extinguish the thin frame of musty willow,
with all its twigs and branches, set afire,
to climb under the moonlight on wild horses,
and wantonly pursue their own desire.

I'm gazing at your eyes, and 'round us trees are waning.
The moon and me reflecting into your eyes profound
... your eyelashes could crush us, as you gaze, absent-minded
but, gently then, my left hand has turned your face around.

sentimental story

Later on, we met more often.
I stood on one side of the hour,
you – on the other,
like two handles of an amphora.
Only words flew between us, back and forth.
Their swirling could almost be discerned,
and suddenly,
I would lower a knee,
and sink my elbow to the ground
only to observe the grass,
tilted by the dive of some word,
as though by the paw of some lion in flight.
The words spun, they spun between us
back and forth,
and the more I loved you, the more
they repeated,
in this whirlpool which is almost envisaged,
the structure of matter, the emergence of being.

nichita stănescu

1933–1983

ballad of the tomcat

A tomcat I desired to be
with upward tail, a stripy coat,
long claws, long whiskers, hissy throat,
with eyes, one green, one brown, you see.

Precisely when the snow of night
towards the sleep of down is creeping,
me, up on top of roofs in flight
the moon will howl in senseless weeping.

Then, seven housewives, devilish spree,
will hurl their seven stones at me
and will, in silence, cuss and weep,
because I howl and stop their sleep.

But from the height of week's disasters,
I'll grin a-howling, dark and vile:
I love the place, and not the masters,
like dogs, who for a bone will smile.

The seven housewives, then, with glee
will hurl their seven stones at me,
and I will howl, and howl anew
until the moon won't be in view.

nichita stănescu

1933-1983

A tomcat I desired to be
with upward tail, with stripy coat,
long claws, long whiskers, hissy throat
with eyes, one green, one brown, you see.

When early rays the day assail,
I'd wander giddy; where to next?
I'd tie a tin onto my tail
to rattle on the streets, perplexed.

Besmirched and tired in a while,
my gut from growling to divert,
I'm gathered up, I spit my bile,
and drag their linen through the dirt.

When on the streets I gallivant,
If rats annoy me with their rant
I'll spit, I'll spit, and then I'll cry
My back I'll camber hard and high.

nichita stănescu

1933–1983

The cats from seven neighborhoods
I'd chase around and to the woods,
a kitten each to cub for me
with eyes, one green, one brown, you see.

Forgotten when I'll die in vain
up near the tavern in the slum
laid in the way of fists to drain
the sour swill, the vile scum.

"Eh... what's a life... out from your tent
let's dance again, don't jump with dread...
look down the drain... and don't lament
the tomcat dead, the tomcat dead..."

yesterday's Sunday

I light up my cigar and wait for you,
Down on the street-bench in the midday sun:
These precious seconds, bright with silver dew
Jiggle like verbs, in jokes without a pun.

The poplars rustle, and in wind unwinding,
Which through my fingers slowly trails away...
And when you're close, the silent shadows binding,
My hand's a lyre, gentle in its sway.

We take small steps to the train station, where,
The platform of our parting we'll refuse:
A remnant of the summer's in your hair,
Your lips are blue of autumn's tardy bruise.

The district dons a dignified attire,
Yesterday's Sunday tied her crown in chains,
Kisses are mute. Sad is the Monday crier.
Farewell to eyes. Farewell small town. The wound remains.

romulus vulpescu

1933-2012

death of the deer

nicolae labiş

1935-1956

The drought killed every breeze, and its fever won't yield,
Sun rays melted on high and have leaked on the field.
All that's left is the sky – empty, hot and forlorn.
Buckets draw filthy mud from the fountains which mourn.
With increasing aplomb from the forests below
Fires dance wild and devilish slow dances of woe.

I follow my father up the old bushy hills,
The pine trees are scratching me, evil and grime.
We have started together on the hunting of deer,
In this hunt born of famine, the Carpathians we climb.
Thirst is crumbling me. On a hot stone flows, boiling
The thinnest of threads creeping down from the well.
My head hangs in gloom on my shoulder. I'm toiling
As if on a planet, dark, vast, strange to tell.

We wait in a place where the waters still sigh;
Rare spring waves, a-strumming on their thin silvery strings.
When the sun will have set, when the moon's in the sky,
In a row, they will come on their path, from afar,
The deer, one by one, for a drink where death stings.

I tell father I'm thirsty; he waves me to be quiet.
Oh, dazzling magic water, how limpid is your sway!
I feel I'm bound, through thirst, to the creature which will die
When law and custom we shall throw away.
What whittled rustle does the valley breathe!

What dreadful evening lingers upon the universe!
Blood spills on the horizon, my breast is read, as if
I wiped my bloody hands on it – a crimson curse.

Ablaze with violet fires, like altars, ferns are burning,
And all the stars, bedazzled, twinkle through them and shine.
How much I wish you wouldn't come, you wouldn't come,
Beautiful offering in these woods of mine!

And vaulting she appeared, and then she stopped
Gazing around as in some kind of fright,
Thin nostrils faintly poised and quivering, on water,
Drew copper circles in the fading light.

Her eyes were shining moist, perplexing, unexplained,
I knew she'd die, she'd hurt, she'd shed a tear.
In me, it seemed, a frightening myth remained,
About the girl who changed into a deer.
From up on high, the pale and lunar light
On her warm fur was sifting a wilting cherry flower.
Oh, how I wished, for just one time, one night,
My father's gunshot hit astray that hour!

Instead, the valley roared.
Down, fallen on her knees,
Her head was tilting upward, towards a gloomy star,
Anon it fell, arising from the water
Elusive swarms of beads, black from afar.
A strange blue bird heaved off between the branches,
My deer's life too, for late horizons meant,

nicolae labiş

1935-1956

Was flying smoothly, like some autumn bird
Absconding her old nest, forgotten, spent.
Under a spell, I went and closed her eyes,
Those shady eyes, beneath her horns, so sad.
Startled, I jumped, all pale and numb, when father
Screamed full of joy: – We now have meat, my lad!

I tell father I'm thirsty, he waves for me to drink.
Oh, dazzling magic water, how gloomy is your sway!
I feel I'm bound through thirst to the creature which died
As law and custom we have thrown away.
But law is all in vain and has no place,
When our lives are hardly keeping pace,
Custom and mercy are but soulless, barren,
As hungry lies my sister, sick, dying in the warren.

From its left nostril father's gun spits smoke
And windless do the leaves run from the oak!
A frightening fire does my father rise.
Oh, how the forest changed, there's no disguise!
From earthly grass, I cup my hands around
A little bell, with silver starry sound...
As from the grill grabs father with his nails
The deer's red heart, and all of its entrails.

So what's a heart? I'm hungry! I want to live, desire...
Oh, do forgive me maiden, my dearest in the fire!
I doze. How tall the fire! The forest, how replete! I cry.
What's father thinking? I eat and cry. I eat!

1935-1956 nicolae labiş

dance

Autumn drowns my soul in plumes of smoke and blue
In my soul bears autumn swarms of leafy bowers.
Sad, this dance of autumn, we will dance anew,
Grim inebriation, softly rocking hours…

Bleeding is the fiddle, black against the mirror.
Thoughts are dead. The will is yielding in atonement.
Without trace or whisper. Only bring me nearer
Arms of empty cosmos, for the passing moment.

Round my eyes are circles. But your eyes are pure.
With so much despairing our steps are rushing!
Like the wind, that's tearing leaves from woods obscure,
Like a wind that's tearing doors from hinges crushing…

By tomorrow morning strangers we'll become,
Silently you'll weep and gaze tomorrow morning
Seeing how through scraggy gardens, empty, numb,
Withered plumes of fog are sounding baleful warning…

You will sit all silent as I did sometimes,
When I wept through autumns, for my love's un-weaving,
And you'll hear the whistle of the wind that chimes
Urging on the clouds, for the horizon, leaving.

While I'll pass beneath the rusty chestnut trees,
Stony lips, pale figure, stealing on the trail,
Rhythmic steps extinguished in the foggy breeze –
Screechy sand remorseful, cowardly to wail…

1935-1956 nicolae labiş

Bessarabia* with sorrow

Strangers into me are pounding
At Wakes or Easters.
And madcap corner me asunder Moldovan** twisters.
Romanians we're not, keeps saying
The stranger constant.
My kin believe him more convincing
Than me, discordant.

Bessarabia with sorrow,
Bessarabia,
Every hill and vale and borough,
Bessarabia!
"Snagged and tangled is your life,"
Bessarabia!
"Like the wheat from hail in strife,"
Bessarabia!

Moldovans pounded me with fury,
Unchristian, evil.
I'm glad, though, that in them Romania
Still finds retrieval.
We're not Romanian, they say, but teary
Their hearts are clinging
When hearing Farcaș, Vicoveanca***
Dolefully singing.

grigore vieru

1935-2009

Bessarabia with sorrow,

Bessarabia!

Every hill and vale and borough,

Bessarabia!

"Snagged and tangled is your life",

Bessarabia!

"Like the wheat from hail in strife",

Bessarabia!

1935-2009 grigore vieru

---

* **Bessarabia** – a province formerly belonging to Romania, after Soviet occupation following
the Second World War – the Republic of Moldova. Much of the population speaks Romanian.
**Moldovan – may refer to members of the refractory pro-Moscow (at the time) regime of the
Republic of Moldova.
*** **Farcaş, Vicoveanca** – Romanian language folk singers.

imaginary age

Who I am, continues to be born.
What I was, is not yet finalized.
I stick my nose through life
Without an intermediary cellophane.
I transfer the gray matter from the left hemisphere
To the right hemisphere,
I bustle with tsunamis and premonitions.
My body has a terribly large number of eyes
And clearly too few arms,
Nothing is quite according to market requirements.
I keep building lights from shadows,
It is me, it is me, it is me,
Shameless as if in bed,
I keep kindling the fire of gossipers.
Who I am, continues to be born,
Who I was, isn't even finalized yet.

1935- riri sylvia manor

Cain

own with the dead lies the word, crushed with dread.
Look! there it is, between rocks scarred and black.
Cursing me, vile, that I left it and fled
the day was dying, the day lay at my back.

I had to crush it, as it climbed over me
that cry of the mountain, black and forlorn
its peak to the heavens was rocking free
I had to catch it at morn.

And at once it was late, and at once it was still
an hour of mist coming down on the world.
I have killed just one word, I have killed just one word
gluey blood on the name is unfurled.

But who dared to set it askew against me
hindering the path of righteousness born?
I have killed to get through, I have killed and got through,
this sword to damnation is sworn.

I don't tremble in fear, I don't tremble but climb
The stairs cut in guilt, fearful, black
I have killed just one word, I have killed it for lying
The day was dying, the day lay at my back.

daniel drăgan

1935-2016

147

marine

Those frightful swamps, the silent shimmer
scent of the night on leafless, empty lanes
watery walkways, reeds and hemlock glimmer
deft poison to keen nostrils, eager veins

I row – a godless hired slave,
conceited to the waving flow
I break from it when it's below
and ripped from magic, rebel knave

I serve another, cheating slave,
my crafty paddle, artful crave
impales with justice, to its grave,
the chest of each and every wave

Those waving swamps, the silent shimmer
they flicker meekly and obey
I'm living in the wave that's coming
and die in that which goes away.

1935-2016 daniel drăgan

all the wattle trees went crazy

All the wattle trees went crazy;
Too much springtime drove them wild,
Flying naked through the heavens,
With their souls on the outside.

They have pulled them out this morning
White and dressed in silver dew;
Strong aromas from the heavens,
Ripped from mysteries anew.

All the wattle trees went crazy,
And their madness seemed to sprout
Something grand and mystifying,
To the world that's blowing out.

Somehow luminous, translucent,
Somehow kinder it will ring,
And somehow this love, accomplished,
Writes a song it wants to sing.

arhip cibotaru

1935–2010

While the flying birds, bamboozled,
Are left breathless, full of scars
As they, vagrantly, glide longing,
Wanderers among the stars.

The green forest, drunk with madness,
Can no longer be kept calm,
As it holds the crescent moon,
Like a heart within its palm.

Can't you see, my soul, which likewise,
With chaotic words it flies,
All the wattle trees went crazy
And you want me to be wise.

the circle

I was walking on the road. There was moonlight, kind of autumn.
And it catches up with me and passes me by
A circle.
A big round thing made of iron.
A circle
Which was going all by itself on the road.
I looked behind: did someone throw it?
Maybe someone pushed it…
Nobody...
And, in the end, who should throw that thing
For it was as big and heavy – as the round rail foot
$\qquad$ of a carriage.

I look ahead: the circle went on its way.
It was moving quickly, quickly and raising up dust.
Just then Calotă's son comes down the hill
– Didja see't man?
– Seen it. And he starts crossing himself.
What is with this, from which barrel did it spring,
Only Spânu has wine barrels so huge,
He might have gone away, and the barrel has toppled.
We were amazed like that, we wondered,
Calotă's son was now white in the face, he got a bit
Scared by
The devilish thing.
And now Gligorie appears.

marin sorescu

1936–1996

– Didja see't man?

– Didn't. What was there to see?

– The circle.

– What circle?

Ghiţă, Calotă's son, bent down and showed him the trace in the dust.

It left a trace like a

carriage wheel.

– Eh, how many wheels pass on this road!

The circle passed like this, aimlessly through the whole village.

Some saw it, some didn't.

Like, out of three near where it passed,

Two saw it, one didn't.

While we were waiting there *Voooo – voo! Ooo!*

Ooo!

Like a great tambourine thing...

And we see clouds of dust...

– Get out of the way, 'cause it's coming... It's going back...

The circle was coming down the hill, perhaps a bit reddened now

From so much running, from so much inspection of the

Bulzeşti village...

It was coming from the village of Prădătorul, having crossed the marshes

through Frăţilă

I grabbed Gligorie's arm:

– D'ya see it man?

– See what?

– The circle.

– What circle?

– This one that is now passing near us!

Don't you hear how the earth is trembling, voooing,

raising dust...

– There's nothing passing. I hear nothing. I see nothing.
The circle came closer... I took a closer look: could I say
That it's like a wheel of a hansom cab? no, 'cause it didn't have spokes...
And it shone too brightly... Like the halo of a saint...
As if the head of some saint was rolling
                              in the dust
And its halo is carrying it like a rail
And it's clothing it in radiance...
It moved whizzing... And it was heating up from so much
                                            rolling,
It was throwing sparks, when it was touching
some stone,
Through Seculeşti, now it was here in Gura Racului,
                              and certainly
It wanted to go downhill to Nătărăi.
I moved closer and I felt its scent:
it smelled like
A perfect round. Like geometry... like cream
                        of geometry,
The essence of essences so to speak...
I fell on my knees.
So lightly and delicately it touched the ground
Full of mud, of the village.
Now it was stepping through Bulzeşti as if it was walking
On the moon, fuckin' thing!
I was shivering with fright and was almost
                              teary,
Of so much honor, so much miracle.

– Eh, now, have ya seen it? – I asked Gligorie,
one more time, who was picking the dirt
                    from under his fingernails

1936–1996 marin sorescu

With a matchstick.

– What's there to see?

– The circle.

– What circle?

– Well then... go back to where you bloody came from, you blind bat!

'Cause I have nothing more to talk with those who see nothing,

apart from

what their wives show them!

– Let's go, I pull Calotă's son's arm...

Lucky you were here... else,

The circle would have told about us throughout the world,

What stupid blind people are in this village.

The story with the fiery circle, coming to inspect,

Circulated a lot in our parts, by word of mouth, from village to village.

Not even the second war succeeded to extinguish it;

Only later, with the transformations˙, it faded

in the background.

And in the end, they prevailed, those who

didn't see it.

˙ **Transformations** – term commonly used to describe the start of the communist period in Romania, circa 1948.

Adam

Although he found himself in paradise,
Adam was walking the alleyways preoccupied and sad
Because he could not quite figure out what was missing.

Then God manufactured Eve from one of Adam's ribs.
And so pleasing was this miracle to the first man
That exactly in the same second
He touched his very next rib,
Feeling his fingertips electrified
By some firm breasts and sweet thighs
As if by some contours of musical tones.
A new Eve had raised before his eyes.
She had just taken her mirror out
And was putting on her lipstick.
"This is life!" – sighed Adam
And he created another one.
And so on, when the official Eve turned her back,
Or was going to the marketplace to buy gold, myrrh, and frankincense,
Adam was bringing to light a new concubine
From his intercostal harem.

God noticed
This frivolous creation of Adam.
He called Adam to him, scolded him with divine cussing
And cast him out of paradise
For surrealism.

marin sorescu

1936-1996

155

the march of Julien the hospitable

ONE happy pilgrim loses his way, singing full of pleasure on the meadows,
with a sweet grape in his purse;
TWO angels kidnap a pancake filled with mint, and every evening
they roll it, passionately on the cross-beams;
THREE angora butterflies fondle, bored, the silky fountains down
the slope where the alleyways converse;
FOUR switchmen wish to burn, in cabins, their similarly perfumed guises,
and all of a sudden their mouths tremble, their fear flowing in streams;
FIVE failed thin girl-students prick – while weeping behind the school,
having their breasts stained with ink – the school holiday with a thorn;
SIX small fringes from the orange curtain in the old vestibule of
the guesthouse are a little torn (but no one is telling);
SEVEN times seven makes forty-nine oranges locked in a warm anthill,
now and forever after;
EIGHT delicate tailors decided, at dusk, to rip the lining of dew from
the fence;
NINE sighs did the blue rose extract from the soup, hot and dense;
TEN is the number at which one dies from laughter!

emil brumaru

1939 –

nightmare

The city square was filled up with the dead,
They crowded out the street, walking asunder
Dressed in their finest clothes, as a reminder
That we, the quick, don ordinary thread.

They passed us laughing loud, with no reserve,
As if they didn't understand one bit
That they were quite a crowd, and didn't fit
Along with us, the living, losing nerve.

We were all frightened by such strange, fantastic script,
And stunned, we stopped to witness this perplexing show
For all of us had someone in the street below
And wouldn't want to leave them locked inside a crypt.

1940– ileana mălăncioiu

love with an empty sack

benone burtescu

1940-2014

I never went hunting in my whole life
And wouldn't want to, though I'd be in big strife.
What would I do if they'd force me one day?
I would wake up quite early and I would kneel to pray:
Give us today, Lord, darkness and fog
Let it rain all day, with lightning and thunder
Daze the hunting dogs and spread them asunder
May the deer stay asleep as if it was deep night
And visit the hunters with terrible fright
May that day sweep fast
And be over at last.

And if this cannot be
I'd still manage, you see.
When the deer would come into view
I would shoot up, or down, or askew,
what a sham!
Even the birds would wonder at how stupid I am
I'd rather shoot myself, that is clear
But I won't shoot the deer.
And I will raise another prayer, still
Carry out, Lord, another miracle, if You will
So that, no matter how long we're on the track
May we return home with an empty sack
But full of love, leave those sweet deer secure.

And we'll find something else to eat, I'm sure.

the tower

And because my enemy told me that I will die
I told him: go mind your own business!
How could you die, Maria?
For it is together, that we've conceived this poem!

And in your heart, you carry the wisdom of all women
As the cross carried Jesus.
Oh, we who threw our happiness away
– Like Joseph by his brothers was thrown –
Only to find that pain is queen!

How could you die, Peter?
You who learned everything by yourself, like Adam,
So that you can be our father, and you painted
When others were killing their parents?
That painting of yours that is called
"The fight against the forces of darkness".
It lead me to believe that if you left,
The planet would follow you like a pure bee!

Or you Mil, how could you die?
When you arrived and started to cry,
Hidden behind the claw of a bird
Thrusting its beak into your right palm.
Or me. How would it be possible for me to die?
When you told me
That tomorrow morning we'd drink coffee,
And we'd open the magazine in which
This poem would not appear.

cezar ivănescu

1941–2008

159

Mil's ballad

Mil, join me at the window, look down and lick your lips,
the street is full of women with mesmerizing hips,
the street is full of women with mesmerizing hips!

you have room by the window, Mil, let's put on our vests:
the street is full of women with splendid looking breasts,
the street is full of women with splendid looking breasts!

come on Mil, do not linger, sit still here in this chair,
the street is full of women with beautiful, long hair,
the street is full of women with beautiful, long hair!

let's go down to the street now, and pray there for a while:
oh Lord let us encounter the one with a lovely smile,
oh Lord let us encounter the one with a lovely smile!

and so, evening by evening, some lucky lad with style,
will stumble upon Death and see her lovely smile,
will stumble upon Death and see her lovely smile!

the brook

A brook I am, all bubbly, fresh and clear
And shaken under summer's starry light
The more the sky is windless, dark and near
The more my chains, astounded, loom in fright

It's not from the outside that rumors scurry
Not from the depths nor from on high
A shadow has detached from glory
In me, its holy icon's set to stay

Increasingly the circles will go deeper
While dances on the waters float away
A bubbling brook has woken up inside me
Can't fill it, nor define it, to this day.

1941–2000 ioan alexandru

balm for the angels

I'm sad, but never sad because of you.
The beasts afraid of wonders run away
Of them, we have forgotten to conceive,
In March and June, August and May.

Bereft of days, who knows? we're passing by
Long childhoods tied around our necks above
While being snowed by holy celebrations,
Not being, being born, falling in love.

What would you give me not to die today?
Balm for the angels, my sad song to play.

constanţa buzea

1941–2012

matter

Matter does not exist. What I now hear,
Like an infinite whisper, overlaid on my being,
Debauched, rampaging, indifferent –
Is nothing but my own collapse.

The gentle violence, precise, red.
A countenance, abstract, drugged.
By everything counting as a drug.
There's no escape, the rest remains as being.
All that once was, all that now screams deep inside its purpose
Fleshy like the flesh, a goal which cannot be attained
A goal driven into the very heart of thought.
High above us. Violence,
Precision, reversing of meaning,
What is good is bad, what is bad
Is my happiness.
My life imagined to myself
To my being disconnected, torn, destroyed.
Melancholia. Suicide is a flower.
It is the possibility. It is the power.

1941 – angela marinescu

the light of midday

- fragment -

On the outskirts of town, on the train rails nearby
I took you with me to look more suave.
Your walk was awkward, on your heels so high
Some passing soldiers called to you for love.

We entered the field on the grazed old grass
Walking 'round the goalposts of opposing teams.
What an effort that was! They feared some misfortune.
Far away from the town, you could hear their screams.

We stopped by the river.
On the shore there were sliding
Long oily moments, impotence, disgust.
And what kind of fish could possibly live there
Or tell me, what questions could be asked?

We paid some attention.
From the station, relentless,
Through hundreds of pipes cried out an appeal.
And since, anyway, someone had to abscond,
All shut themselves inside with a seal.

We were left in the field, like two odd exceptions.
Suddenly strangers and feeling ashamed.
You avoided my gaze, and somehow I suspected
That there, in the field, we will both be condemned.

1941-2008 adi cusin

the roof

It so happens that I was passing by,
after many years, through my village
and I stumbled in front of the house
where I was born (now it belongs to someone else)
exactly at the time
when someone, perched upon the roof
covered with old square clay slates
was breaking them off, slowly,
replacing them with some red tiles.

He had no idea
that he was skinning
a few heavens from above me,
and the scream could not be heard either.

He was just changing some
square clay slates, now too old,
with some new red tiles.

ion pop 1941–

autumn, leave my trees all green

Autumn, leave my trees all green,
Here, I give you both my eyes.
Yellow winds blew in last evening
Kneeling woods were wet with cries.

Autumn, leave my sky untouched
Lightning-strike my forehead, please.
Late last night the whole horizon
Tore itself up in the breeze.

Autumn, leave my air with birds,
Drive away my steps from me.
For at morn, the blue has drained
Screams of larks, an endless plea.

Autumn, leave me grass and leave me
All the fruit, and leave
Bears un-sleepy, storks un-flying
Luminescent eve.

Autumn, leave me light and don't
Weep the sun a-smoke today.
Set your evening on me now,
I'm eve anyway.

1942 - ana blandiana

166

we should

We should be born old,

We should arrive wise,

Be capable of deciding our fate in this world,

To know, from that primordial crossroad, what roads are commencing

And only the longing to journey deemed irresponsible.

Later we should become young, younger still, travelling,

Mature and strong we should arrive at the gate of creativity,

Enter through it into love, entering it as adolescents,

And become children, when our children are born.

Anyway, by then they should be older than us,

Could teach us how to talk, could rock us to sleep,

We would disappear little by little, progressively growing smaller,

Like a grain of wheat, like a grain of mustard, like a grain of sand...

1942 – ana blandiana

in Paris

In Paris at corner gates
Cherries grow inside their crates;

While the grapes, to knock your socks
Grow for you ripe in a box.

Peaches, who could have believed?
Wrapped in tissue, grow relieved.

And believe me, when I say:
Apples grow in shops all day.

Plums on weighing scales grow well,
As do melons, can't you tell?

Strawberries, though somewhat rushed
Grow on stalls already washed.

And the peanuts, true and true,
Grow in pubs out of the blue.

Quite a bore inside this city,
Not a bee, and not a kitty.

Still, there's something hard to beat:
In Paris, on every street,

Around the doggies' tails, alert,
Grow baguettes and camembert.

1942 – ana blandiana

168

you shall hear again: be my heart

you shall hear again: be my heart

it's simple: you just open some canals

which out of habit wouldn't lead anywhere

then you burn your clothes

a skin feverishly unbuttoned

human

tomorrow or the day after only his witness, perhaps remembrance

with its brotherly chaos: an even smaller giant my heart and

therefore you become my second

heart

come closer

to all this, what will you reply? without a word

you will leave the city tonight

and in your absence: a scar on a wall of air

getting smaller by the minute

virgil mazilescu

1942–1984

this taffeta lot

Nor blue, neither flame
the colorless chant
belongs to a frame
that's poached by an ant.

Both yellow and pink
so-so in its tone
no creeds to rethink,
no deeds to atone.

Part olive, part bay
with color subdued
it doesn't rely
on starting a feud.

Now gray and now rose,
this taffeta lot
one could say it's yours
but maybe it's not.

1942 – șerban foarță

against war

Civilian things are few, there's no reprieve
These rainy times with soldiers beating drums
We don't have days, just military leave,
And babies jump saluting from their mums

The clocks resound like soldiers' boots this morning
They screech on jilted, barren sand which stings
For thirty wars start monthly without warning
And all are bearing death within their wings

And even death has lost its charm and poise
These rainy times of drills and conscript days
Beneath the linden trees the arms make noise
While stars are gunning us with death-filled rays

adrian păunescu

1943-2010

It's easy to acknowledge, though it rankles,
For like a yoke you feel it on the way,
The fact that from one's conscience to one's ankles
A man is just a uniform today.

Civilian things are scarce and hard to tell
For even heartaches lack civilian beat
And stern recruitment seems to augur well
For sheepish tame civilians in defeat

But troopers smile! It's resurrection mass,
When babies jump saluting from their mums
As per the statute to address their brass
In rainy times with soldiers beating drums.

legal division

The mystery of love and of dying,
What more can I tell about us
But since we part ways now, my darling,
The world can be split without fuss.

All legal divisions will follow
All heartaches for all it is worth,
The lawyers will skin all that's civil
I take to the south, you the north.

Since all will be evenly parted,
Just give me the night, take the day.
Just give me the death, you keep living
Division is fair in this way.

Our wonder was mirrored in heaven,
The last time we flew over hope
One wing you shall carry as luggage,
The other I'll drag on a rope.

1943-2010 adrian păunescu

173

No evidence will I need ever,
No witnesses – honest or true,
Enough that in all court's decisions
My fact and my witness are you.

Take mountains and leave me the valleys
Take sunlight and leave me the night
For what is there left to behold now,
Since losing your eyes from my sight?

The way of partition shall thus be:
You take all you want, all you know
Forget not one last thing behind you
And take me along as you go.

the illusion of an island

Tonight we depart for the shore of my island,
the coach made of walnut is waiting, my dear,
remember to take some warm clothes and a garland,
and rush, for police dogs are wont to appear.

Don't worry about it; the driver is dead,
the horses are dead too, and so is the carriage,
we'll run with no trace to the harbor of dread,
to my five headed island, awaiting our marriage.

We'll raise ugly children on that island that festers,
while steel branded butlers laugh dirt through their gills,
they'll bore us with stories of long-gone ancestors,
with splashing wet corpses, with telegraph drills.

We'll take many pictures but only for show,
to send them away for the world to observe,
like marbles we'll spread their three eyes in the snow,
The Fourth Eye we'll keep for the house and preserve.

The whole day we'd wander, bare-skinned, without flaw,
on fiery sleighs, we will fly through the skies,
and I, like a farmer, am striving to sow
some wheat, sweet and idle, reposed on your thighs.

1943–2010 adrian păunescu

175

I'm waiting, for now... It's the middle of summer,
or the middle of winter, how strange is this story;
don't speak, for the climb in the chill makes you stammer,
but the carriage seems dead, so why should you worry?

It's just an illusion, I'm over the fence,
with four thousand candles I'm waiting for you,
don't fret, for the white snow is just a pretense,
and the house guards keep mute and a-smoke in our view.

Step up – do not linger, come sing me a song,
the driver is suitably dead for our marriage,
no witnesses wait on the island, no throng,
my suit is of walnut, I'm almost a carriage.

My face I just found, if it's gone by the morning,
it might be a gale, a tempest which looms,
for I am the mound of the freshest of tombs
and frosty your step will become without warning!

And so this is all, we're departing at last.
The ghost of the carriage grins mute from the past.

Mioritic* nostalgia

I yearn

for a still starry night

with my homeland's meadows in my sight,

the rainy smell on fresh hay and damp scrub,

and the happy naked baby in his tub.

I yearn for the corn fields of childhood,

for Dan's valley with frosty grey bunches of grapes,

for the sunny lane of Albele –

full of children, who merrily traipse.

I yearn

for a bitter cherry tree in flower,

for the kids of those moments

whom I nimbly pursued in that happy hour.

I yearn for the Black Sea,

for a holiday with waves in the sun

for the moon rising,

near The Casino**, from the sea spray,

for a concert at The Athenaeum***,

on New Year's Day.

---

* **Mioritic** – describing the Romanian territory straddling the Carpathian Mountains; related to *Miorița*, popular national ballad of Romania, regarded as describing the national ethos.
** **The Casino** – famous architectural building on the edge of the Black Sea in the city of Constanța; former casino and tourist attraction.
*** **The Athenaeum** – one of Bucharest's architectural highlights and concert hall.

1943 – lidia săndulescu-popa

I yearn

to row a boat again

on my heart's lake

one summer in the Herăstrău* park,

for the garden with beehives, from where father

would bring sheaves of lilies

every Friday evening, before dark.

I yearn

for a princess in the castle of Bran**,

for the Old Ladies from Bucegi***,

for the cross on the Caraiman****,

I yearn for linden trees in flower,

which my street still adorn.

I yearn for me,

For my homeland, I yearn!

---

lidia săndulescu-popa

1943 –

* **Herăstrău** – the largest public garden in Bucharest.
** **Bran Castle** – famous medieval castle in Romania, known by tourists as "Dracula's castle".
*** **The Old Ladies (Babele) from Bucegi** – a rock formation in the Carpathian Mountains resembling a group of ladies standing and chatting in a circle.
**** **The cross of Caraiman** – huge metal structure in the form of a cross, raised on the top of Caraiman mountain in the Carpathians, to commemorate the soldiers fallen in the First World War.

ballad of that chatterbox Coquette

It was sometime in April, I remember
perhaps in nineteen seventy and... what...
my soul was full of bones like crimson ember
buried in fear and boredom, and all that;

and at the Mongol's inn, in shadow's beauty
with good old wines, and scents, and no regret,
there came a time I had to pay my duty
of love towards that chatterbox Coquette.

Beneath the sunset of her eyebrows parting
I yearned for my first worship to progress,
from which her mouth would lazily be starting
the nightly bud of passion to undress.

She carried in her eyes a sad carnation
which lingered on the seconds passing by,
and thus proclaimed my fall into temptation
with teary fingers, twilighting the sky.

horia bădescu

1943 –

But where's the cockle shell her ear was forming,
which rested on her temples' sleepy tress?
And where, for her, my voice arose performing
a poet's songs, a velvety caress?

And where, the rounded shape, and languid frailty
of words, for which we oftentimes would pine
and where, her bosom, vanquished, shy and dainty
and where her lovely ankles' starry shine?

And where, her thighs' angelic adumbration
And where is her surrender's white egret?
Oh where, the hour, cast beyond creation,
Of love towards that chatterbox Coquette?

lied

The world beyond of beyond
the line of the horizon.
Hunger for you
and the hands of autumn
rummaging through the garbage cans of the sunset.
One step, another one
through the blood of crucified maples;
at the other end of town
Mary Magdalene wipes off the dirty window of the day
with her breasts.

a handsome groom I stride in death

in Heaven's algebra, my mind is cast
to every thought, I have assigned a name
through abstract precepts, I forget my past
and wedded by the spring, my bride I'll claim
a handsome groom I stride in death again

without my body, I am my last flower
to learn the unseen from its vast domain
while my soul is a wandering path every hour

together, my love, we shall sail through the skies
and close to You, Lord, we will linger anew
we shall live in our words full of spirit and wise

we'll return to the world like falls passing through
to ripen the song of the grape in the womb
to fill with the skies this mystery's bloom

aurel buricea

1943 –

the bewilderments of Moses

What flames, Sir, what flames,
And how that fire never ceased
And how there was no smoke,
As if from within itself it was burning
And in itself existence rested.

What a staff, Sir,
And how it mocked Pharaoh's serpents,
And his painted sepulchers,
How it swallowed their words from between their lips
Until their lies spurted through their nostrils.

What seas I parted with it,
What roads I pierced through the desert,
What stars illuminated its point
And what an umbrella it became through the day.

What stones, Sir, what stones,
What fine cutting,
How the words sparkled –
The letter and the sun,
The jot and the star.

petre anghel

1944–2015

What holy ark, Sir, what an ark,

What short-circuit once a year,

What miracle from a few twigs

So that even today the place remains unknown

Amongst the unending questions of the mind.

Everything has gone,

Everything is forgotten,

Nothing was saved.

Only your voice

Was worthy,

When you said:

This one will not pass to the other side,

And the dust will not cover him,

He will be taken with me.

early in the morning

Gift me your smile as if you were gifting me
a house with walls made of glass.
So that I can see the brook gurgling under
the light-made bricks of the roof
to watch the flowering of the sternum bones
the upward road of bliss
and the spring buds of the word
telling stories about the regained wisdom
of the Sunday.

The jail as well as the palace
the mud as well as the stars
the win as well as the loss
the plain as well as the hill

Gift me your smile as if you were gifting me
a house with walls made of glass
a cross, on which to crucify myself
forever and ever, amen.

1944– vasile igna

the burning phase

Situated somewhere oscillating variable
Between the electronic microscope
And the Hubble telescope,
Between the Princess of Monaco's gown and
Fetuses, chrysalides of the angels, between
Tsunamis, volcanoes, Schuman's resonance and
The experiment of mutation, globalization
The new primordial after the day
All time packed into a single NOW
All cemeteries for one single Reabsorption.
And only She, Pulsation,
Inside the innermost of snowing,
Inside the sphere of orgasm,
And only He,
Rainbow of the night,
The stars stay there even during the day,
The sun is still there
Even at night.

eugen evu

1944 –

creation

After about six days
of pottering under the spherical flight
of the Holy Ghost
He was about to give up,
and instead of forming the clay, almost,
just gave it the transparency
of the living one -
but now it resembled more and more
the human image of the Son.
On the left, his heart had been singing
with a wave from a sigh to another sigh,
but something was missing there,
one abyss seeking another for symmetry
and on his right side, firmer,
like a kiss on the dried clay awaiting,
extinguishing itself on the vessels.
"Hide the pain of your sadness,"
with a sigh said the Son,
"that I may carry it in My cup made of mud,
and when man will pierce The Man
it will pour out water and blood!"

dumitru ichim

1944 -

farewell letter

george ţărnea

1945-2003

What multitudes between us now, my dear,

Numbering rains in pairs, if far or near,

And from a longing eye, aloof, unknown,

How many snows on our lips have grown...

Listen to me and then just let me cry

I fear the dark, the cold, I can't deny

And I don't want to know who, in the end,

Has beautifully loved, who love misspent,

Who first stepped out at night, who went away,

Who left the game, and who was left in play,

Who pulled at walls to wreck them one by one,

Whose days, in thought, returned where they began,

Who's on the winning side and who has lost,

Who's bound, and who away the shackles tossed,

Who in the other with more faith confided

And under skies too strange, too high, was guided,

When I forget your voice and its sweet verse,

Apart from silence, what can I find worse

And how can I beneath the stars find rest,

Since I have lost your shadow from my breast?

Numbering rains in pairs, if far or near,

What multitudes between us now, my dear.

the island of happiness

We all try to survive
in this century of turbulence
creating small islands in our imagination
where we escape when we
can no longer cope
with the hurricanes and earthquakes
which assail us.
There,
on our island
we play hopscotch
even if our hinges are giving way,
we coo like babies,
we sit on the emperor's throne
without fear of punishment,
we kiss and we love
together with all the intangible stars
of the modern world.
There,
on the island of our happiness,
it is forever spring.

george roca

1946–

There,

we too are eternally young

and healthy

and joyful

and… good!

Sometimes,

when on our island of happiness

we feel lonely,

we invite, of course,

dear friends

to join us

and to share in our joys.

And so,

a miraculous symbiosis is created

which heals the soul

of all the Earth's ills

making you think with clarity

when you return to reality.

thorns

You adorned me

With flowers stolen from the garden of Gethsemane.

And a porcelain vessel broke

In the storeroom full of young cattle carcasses.

The fattened calf proved to be skinny

And my fingers keep wandering

Between the keys of the blood colored harpsichord.

How can I feed all the relatives,

Who gathered together at the wedding

From the seven times seven winds?

The family restaurant went bust,

And one by one

Hungry and thirsty,

We pluck thorns from under the fingernail

With which

I am ready to dig into the fat humus.

The olive trees grow the unction

Black like the apron

Which plumps up over the womb of another carpenter's woman.

melania cuc

1946–

mythology

Alas, one day – but when precisely?
Our souls got lost out of the blue
Leaving behind only enigmas
As in the ancient land of U.

We, being poor, have gathered, waiting
For tidings under skies, and stagger
To sell ourselves to Melancholy
Loved by creation's heavy dagger.

And as we're dreaming under blood pines
About white sails, every so oft
Alas, arrived, by salt eroded
A small papyrus, dim, aloft.

We doubted it, and hoped for further
Tidings anew, but they've forgotten
To bring to us the major news
As if we all were guilty, rotten.

dan verona

1947 –

Alas, one day – but when precisely?
Our souls got lost out of the blue
Leaving behind only enigmas
Like in the ancient land of U.

This emptiness we feel so burning
As if at midnight sweet noon's dawning –
As in her son a mother patterns
An age with pure, eternal fawning.

Our mouths are parched, and there's no dew
From eden, trees have long now gone
Beneath a hollow full of honey
As absaloms, we dream alone.

Past sailors, cast away by seas,
Same seas which in the sky we feel
But still, with patience we keep waiting
While wearing heavy crowns of steel.

dan verona

1947 –

193

the parcel

He was schoolmate, a parcel I think
Living safely in a postman's house
Didn't spit saliva but was speaking ink
And throughout the city, he was stepping stamps

While his gaze was dripping telegrams each morning
Leaning on his shoulder, or his other chest
And we butchered him with our glare, so burning
Like a tender laser, perfect in its quest.

Now the rain was heavy, chestnut trees were breaking
And in town we walked with Satan for a quid,
While hot Annie's hair turned white as she was shaking
When he kindly asked us:
Won't you close that lid?

flower of frost

Flower of frost, shining bright on my window,
Your image blooms lifeless on the glassy slice,
Born from a blue night, cold on my pillow,
In which I, too, was transformed into ice.

Flower of frost, shivering, wintry,
Reaching from a white and heavenly grove,
Pray don't come near my outstretched fingers,
Else you might thaw, and might melt on their stove.

Flower of frost, without a fragrance,
Without a stem, and without any clay,
May you forever be a bride through the darkness,
A word or a syllable, tender, astray.

Flower from heaven, you belong in winter,
Flower from heaven, I belong in autumn.
You hear the blizzard, how sweet its clamor!
Urging to part us, to have us forgotten.

Flower of frost, knocking faint at my window,
Your image shines gently on the glassy slice,
Risen from a snowfall bluer than sapphires,
In which I, too, was snowing with ice.

adrian popescu

1947 –

burn

The flesh on my body is all a candle,
I'm a flame, and to the limpid sky I strive,
And like the birds, dead
I shall weigh heavier than alive.

The burning eye is feeding on the wax
And it begets a drop of scalding dew
One time I knew how to fly, one time,
I've no proof, but I recall it's true.

My entire body is now a candle
For after it will drain in the dirt of the land
And its flame will melt down into blue
You will still feel a burn on your hand.

1947 – adrian popescu

all men

All men
Who passed through my heart
Some rushing,
Others lingering for a while –
Could return today, even,
At least
To leave a kiss on my forehead.
All men
Because of whom
My heart is often pale
Could enter
On one of these pages
On the occasion of this celebration.
Maybe even one of them could admit
That my shadow was comfortable for him
(And he, at last, learned something, for sure),
And then he could take his destiny in his hands
Fastened to my breast
Like a safety pin.

All men,
I want all those I've had,
Some young and joyful,
Some already dead…
To forgive me when, madly, I cry
For my droplet of air,
For my handful of the sky.

renata verejanu

1947–

and the only visibility of time

and the only visibility of time was the wind
through the branches outside

bringing, sometimes, with the fingers of a child,
the rumble of the river
down from the alders

the clouds passed with whispering flakes
on the adolescent figure of the mother

to her, maternity was gifted,
like, out of the blue, the snowing

three oranges were quivering by the window
in the intermediary cold

a new innocence was possible

and while the remembering was suckling its forgetfulness
life continued

dinu flămând

1947 –

minuet

Tonight there's a ball in the oval saloon
slip on your dancing shoes my Cinderella
with pink crinoline and a silky umbrella,
for queens made of gold will line up your parade
and knights in white armor will provide your arcade
the orchestra, laced in a silvery net,
will tempt us to dance a sweet minuet,
as with sapphire glances, I'll be dazzling you
when, with grace, our dance we'd be starting anew.
With perfumes discrete and with laces replete
you sail through the warmth of the air in full moon
tonight, at the ball, in the oval saloon.
and shortly thereafter, in the dead of the night,
when soft music sways us in whispered delight,
you won't run away, like the fairy tale swears,
since I finished to spread the pitch on the stairs
so linger a while, Cinderella my love,
as my hand, seeking yours touches your glove,
to take it and kiss it in an amorous chase
for I see on your foot the slipper of glass
in the end, the moon with a faint olive ray
beholds through stained windows this tender display
while we're mourning the orchestra, dead, with no tune.
Oh how sad is this ball
in the oval saloon!

1947 – george stanca

a moment's sonnet

adrian munteanu

1948 –

I write a sonnet. Consummate delusion
That through some canon I shall freely strive.
I am my wish, my knowing, and my drive,
A modest cobbler scribing love's conclusion.

In some dark corner, dizzy lies my thought
And I can't find its frail elucidation.
I'm stuck inside its contrary fixation
And into murky worlds I'm thrown and caught.

Imploring voices beg for pathless trails
But others howl, stand ready to seduce
With purple vistas like in grand old tales.

When, sanctified by secret verbs, I'm aching
Of me I don't remember, empty scales.
Profound manifestation that I'm waking.

tell me my darling where is your repose

Tell me my darling where is your repose?
In harebrained nests, by waxing evening tide?
Where do you set your feet, so they abide
The searing traces in their dying throes?

How did you keep in check your savage cry
Which cleaves through forests, softly in its stride,
So that I kneel anew and lie beside
The deep, sweet, shadow of your maiden thigh?

Put down your crown onto the blood-red grass,
Go drink sweet nectar from the frosted grail;
Past ardent lips let living water pass,

Burn up your raiment in a fiery gale,
For you are pure, and I shall say a mass,
Your beauty on this altar to unveil.

1948 – adrian munteanu

intermediary age

I'm thirty-three years old, my Lord,
for crucifixion ripe and wise,
accomplished on this cross to hang,
on which the perfect verses rise;

this poem, which so simply could
the winter for a spell defer.
I'm castigated for a blunder
which only later I'll incur.

Rebellion of this blood of mine,
it softens in my parents' vein.
But where is Judas to betray me
for thirty silver coins to gain?!

The dusk is spreading over walls,
a rosy moss, grown in some spree;
as death is near, and gently winks,
I'm learning still to be, to be...

nicolae dabija

1948 –

nothing else

Yellow leaves, like defeated birds,
innocent –

the autumn, on the Prut river, has triumphed
such as the old woman from eighteen twelve,
who isn't so sure anymore
how she was born, where and when she died.

And again it seems like winter,
people made of mud and grains
startled, bewildered –
northern ghosts are keeping watch
to stop the running of Moldova back into Moldova.

And the autumn and death keep asking:
why, Lord, around here
nothing else is happening, save for
the transfiguration of the season?…

dumitru băluţă

1948 –

diptych – Lolita 1/17

... The werewolf was a dreamer and sorcerer kin of the magi
while Sinai's crimson sun in the twilight
the star of desire and perseverance (from these two the world is composed,
even!) forgoes descending
and starts to climb higher and higher – specifically
to its predestined sunset
while in a succession of balconies, rococo of Morocco
the sybarites' successions of lives were lifting goblets
(I beg your pardon: glasses with tea!)
for the past and future one thousand and one nights;
all the while
I was conceding, like Adam, antecedent to the review
of the history of Middle Asia
fixed in the world's memory like a scraping together of mirages
inclusive of the famous fruit garden
which gave the world an ongoing headache –
and it would take a considerable amount
of post-biblical time until every attempt
of mysterious connivance for de-conspiring of thinking
but mostly of man and everything that's his – Hallelujah! – like
a failure of philosophy recognized by himself in
the humdrum sliding of senses on the wind rose vectors
and of Rosa Trahtenberg – an anonymous
who continues to repeat in an almost Eminescian* fashion:
philosophy – insanity.

---

* **Eminescian** – in the manner of Eminescu, Romania's national poet.

leo butnaru

1949 –

the destiny of those who love their nation

To brother Grigore[*]

Our Easter's here, Grigore, of the meek,
An Easter just as gentle as you are
And in my life, not days, but hours I seek
To die, to resurrect, most painful scar.

How beautiful and gentle is this spring
I do regret it, in some corner curled
My life has scattered wildly, like some fling –
A stranger's every poet in this world.

They call us strangers; us, who not just once
Romanians against strangers have defended,
But now we are rewarded like some dunce;
In brothers' curse, despicable we've ended.

They howl from some satanic thirst for power,
They cuss us, who for liberty have yearned
And who against machine-guns did not cower
But jumped out from exploding cars which burned.

leonida lari

1949–2011

---

[*] Leonida Lari dedicates this poem to Grigore Vieru, fellow poet and kindred soul in the struggle for the rights of the Romanian population in the Republic of Moldova.

They cursed us Grig, for how the hell we're found
Pursued in winter or in spring, like game,
We're not to parties or to interests bound,
But to the country and its godly flame.

Tell me, my brother, for my mind does weaken
From all these devilish nets without a rest,
In Chișinău we're spat on, scoffed and beaten,
And beaten once again in Bucharest?

It's clear my brother, perfect sense it makes,
These God-forsaken traitors stoop so low,
For the same hand is mixed in all the scrapes
In Bucharest, as well as in Chișinău.

The same hand writes their lies in the same papers
Anti-Romanians all, an evil heist,
We're international, they say, the traitors
Who bring into this world the Antichrist.

The Easter of the meek is here, and pure
Respect is paid to dead ones, strangers too,
How beautiful this spring is, how demure
In which among the meek we'd be anew!

We'd walk through parks, streets, markets, in disguise
Becoming like the mob, crumpled and torn,
How often we've faced death, gazed in its eyes,
While around us an empty space would form.

An emptiness, a vacuum for defense,
Began somewhere from the Arhei direction,
A strange old wheel, a guise, a mood intense
Which seems to save ideas, bring protection.

... Bright Easter candles burn a lonely light
 On lonely graves at Dniester's craggy shore
Where dead lay our country's best and bright,
Sent without weapons in a bloody war.

They have been sent into this slipshod war,
Mindlessly started without any goal,
The capital was spared the blood and gore,
Which paid on Dniester's bank a crimson toll.

leonida lari

1949–2011

Brother Grigore, I'm ablaze in pain,
My soul's in rage with a demented fire,
For while our young were for the country slain,
The tzars for rum and vodka would retire.

They would laugh loud, some silly joke they'd quack,
And janissaries over them would guard,
When children's bones under the tanks would crack,
Their blood, to heaven, groans and cries bombard!

I am repulsed by this old world my brother,
Which even heaven's circle can't defend,
For one would fight for freedom; while another
Will always choose an easy, worthless, trend.

Our Easter's here, Grigore, of the meek,
And death I lack, and life is not my station –
Our lives do not for days, but hours seek
The destiny of those who love their nation.

somewhere in Venice

I dreamt I was in Venice.
That I was 20 again
and lightning was my brother.

On my scarf, strange signs
a heavenly hand was painting.
My hair had the scent of mandarins
my breasts smelled like just-ripened lemons.
And I was staying at a small hotel with a faded sign.

On the wharf at dawn, I was waiting for you.
You were the merchant of pearls and myrrh.
Your lips had the scent of apples stored in the hay,
your cheeks were wearing the salt of tears mixed
with seas and oceans.

You were always arriving in the month of May
after one, two or three years of absence.
And I kept asking you always the same thing:
"Where have you been for the last two hours?"

liliana ursu

1949 –

The gondola in which you took me for a paddle
you were piling with azaleas, with freesias and with birds red and blue
with our bodies drunk with love.
With the supreme sensuality of the stars, from our palate.

You never said anything.
And so your journeys were replacing words, for me
and sometimes even life.

Whenever you left, I would return to my small Venetian room.
I would play chess all by myself
would paint long scarves
with more and more complicated patterns.
And in the evening, in the small white ceramic fireplace
I would burn long letters.

1949 – liliana ursu

encore repetition

Years of "soups, broths, prams"
washed dishes, salaries,
general cleanings,
wisdom gained on the run
randomly
Years of blind adoration
of credulity
Years of aprons around the waist,
of torn stockings
under melancholy dresses,
Years like flower buds, pale
and of betrayals
Years full of the pain of life, of death,
rosy dreams, hopes aglow,
inspired and unstoppable years
covered in love…
All of these have disappeared
remonstrating.

angela mamier nache

1949 —

elegy for frigid trains

If you would sleep my darling, on railway tracks one morning
the blushing trains would whisper on tiptoes while you're still,
huge bales of cotton-candy the sky will be adorning
we'd all be drunk with dew milk and dancing a quadrille

An angel will be coming from high and ancient railways
to iron out your sleep time with peacock feathers light
and large sequoia forests they'll plant on lonely byways
in markets to spread gratis soap bubbles big and bright

Your hair of early sun rays will conquer cold Siberias
for snow to sizzle slowly on ostrich heads in suits
and then in frigid barracks your eyelashes in series
will linger on damp pillows of teary young recruits

But you don't sleep, my darling, on railways old and shoddy
where filthy trains pass daily, with charcoal dusty, fake
they miss the perfect beauty, a maiden's sweet fresh body
and for their sake I'm weeping, I'm crying in their wake

mircea dinescu

1950 –

Pilate – the man

The lions drained through the sand's placenta,
the monkeys perished due to monkey sadness...
They could reappear in a thousand years
like little beetles reappearing from under the drunkard's table,
The wind will carry seeds of orange trees and flamingos,
The typhoon will spread the pollen of giraffes,
we will eat watermelons
and instead of seeds we shall spit salamanders and squirrels
Nature will remember
the sweet amnesia of time will melt,
the power stations will produce fish and grass,
the lightning will suck on lamps with the greediness of calves
The Father will seek forgiveness
From the Son
But I fear, oh I fear that Pilate – the man
will again wash his hands of it all.

mircea dinescu

1950 –

213

ludic

There are some instincts left, too big for a computer
There are some feelings left uncodified.
The soul yearns after an illicit body
Such as a stream with banks unedified.

At discount price they sell one gram of hope,
While skeptically we're watching from the Square
Where prudent saints methodically consume
Their halos with determined flair.

The bull returns once more to the arena
From ancient times, charmed, mythical, unreal.
Let's hit him with a laser beam this evening
Or with a tired atom's wheel.

Who, these days, for the lion's den is meant?
Who wastes their time on gestures anachronic?
Who still consumes the linden flower's scent
In this age precise and ironic?

daniela crăsnaru

1950 —

You smile as if encoded between meetings,
Between two heart attacks, your roll calls fit
And hide with care between your folds of flesh
An instinct insolent and obsolete.

Bizzare, a chart methodically invites you,
While staying human, guiltless to remain.
That's why this year your thought permits one minute
Of tenderness adulterine again.

When in the mood, in Eden I scrub floors,
My life's ablaze beneath a ludic scepter,
Deep, under boiling cellared vowels which are,
For succulent and lewd words, the receptor.

skipping rope

You have a single skipping rope over which you skip,

The rope draws about your head the line of a tabernacle

And when you jump above it, beneath your soles it draws perfectly a tabernacle

You can boast

You can scold

The pharaohs laying stiff in their graves

And so what, and so what

If you boast about the granite

You no longer jump from death to life

Nimble soles

The scalp in flight, like the tip of an arrow

On the tree bark with my fingernail, I will scratch

My name,

So that my name will grow too,

Just as swaddled, grow the mummies.

the return of the father

cassian maria spiridon

1950–

1. My father was running
   through swamplands
   with the horse
   much too heavy
   for his back
   so old
   I cannot help but laugh
   through the big swamp
   the old lame man
   runs alone
   I am far away
   shame on you
   you laugh, you sing
   be merry brothers
   your father is returning
   from prodigality
   and I will kill him
   for the great feast
2. My father sick
   yellow spiky
   carries his steps
   through the mire
   he doesn't understand me
   I do not understand him
   – is it night already
   or is it not –

me... you...

You
are the autumn
in which I was born
from abysses gathered in my soul.
I
am your season
in which gestures ripen
and gazes harvested at twilight.
You
are my hourglass
without time.
I
am the silence resounding
in hollow monasteries.
You
are the dream.
I
am the corollary.
You
are the wonder.
I
am the pain.
You
are the seed.
I
am the forbidden fruit.

The autumn sifts yellow
sunsets painfully
on the cheeks of this rain.

lelia mossora

1951 –

late I am

Late I am, and for the crushing hour I brood,

Samson without eyes, slowly propelling my destiny's wheel.

The world's old axle, into my bosom screwed,

Unborn child, abandoned on dry seas, in a fisherman's creel.

Weeping alone, beside the post of this nefarious temple

Of all the world's gods, vacuous, atheist, slight,

Under shattered arches, I shall crush them all,

Worshippers and dagons, sorry sight.

As for my plight, the line is drawn and nothing's at stake.

My new sideburns, You take!

I don't deserve new eyes, as mine I have melted on rubble

Only Your name I still have, as for mine I don't trouble,

For Your rays, I'll await, under ruins, which shall be my hearse.

Avenge me, my Lord, with this kamikaze old verse.

1952- Florin Iáiu

the registers of Golgotha (1)

The Registers of Golgotha are close to our domain
You see, the walls, dark crimson, with blood and pain are painted
The wound of this humanity in nightly sighs has fainted
The crucified are weeping, and both awake again.
The entrance through the rear and angels guard each season
They keep forever filling those secret records, cursed.

The crucified are anguished with coldness and with thirst
While registers are reeking of vinegar and treason.
The hallway to the coffins is teeming to the brim
From Jesus' day, no changes have happened, in the main;
Like then, the treason section has disappeared again
But the delighted angels keep working in fine trim.
The registrar is daily awarding them their pay
With Judas' silver coin, forever to betray.

arcadie suceveanu

1952 –

air with diamonds

She was so beautiful that
the old retiree
started to gnaw at the upholstery
of the chair where she sat on the bus.
The bus reached toward her
with the mouth of the carburetor
attempting to tear her dress off.
The chewed up drivers wept over the munched steering-wheel
because she was out of reach –
In return, she was so beautiful
that even the dogs scoffed
the bitumen under her soles.

When she entered the house without a name
 the doorman swallowed his decorations
and the mechanic broke with his teeth
the wrench and the cable
of the elevator which carried her
to the last floor.
The quadriplegic with the social-merit order
started to gobble the useless door-handle
and the naked lock
through which a luxury baby pram
could not flow.
All of them ate
the foot of the attic
all of them ate

florin iaru

1954 –

the roof tiles
when she climbed fluttering on the roof
when she could no longer be reached.
The weatherman on the mountain of
Golgotha
chewed at the weather predictions
and the last
Man in
Cosmos
devoured his capsule
when she exited the earth's atmosphere.
–

What will you do now in the heavens?
they asked her
their mouths dripping with regrets.
But she was so beautiful that she remained beautiful
from then on too.

And they could not find in the whole world
in the whole wide world
enough teeth
enough throats
in which to crush
to grind and to ram
the forever growing distance
and the rest of the words until death.

Florin Iaru

1954–

the timber warehouse

Shadows on high, clouds like a conversation of no one
to nowhere.
More tattered than a letter from the war-front,
my blood
will one day catch up to my heart.

With eyes closed, fists clenched, knees
to my chin,
one fine day
I will behold the world, I will touch it surprised, I will traverse it far away!
Young – I wished to see the pyramids – young,
through the open window I saw the wire fence
of the timber warehouse.
It is warm in there and the sawdust still remembers your steps.
It is cold in there and the watchman sometimes talks in his sleep
about better times.

Sadder than the sound of axes,
more joyful than the saw blades, between saw-mills,
I thought that I see your window catching fire.
Glued to the aromatic timber-slats
I warmed my hands at the flame of your hair.

traian t. coşovei

1954-2014

You, who read between your fingers the flowing phrases of clouds,
you, who wanted to look at the pyramids between your fingers –
with eyes closed, with fists clenched, knees
to your chin,
take shelter inside its warm haze for one night,
get lost inside its stony depth
even if for just one night!

One day the timber warehouse will burn.
One day my life will ascend, full of light.

traian t. coşovei

1954-2014

a description of the South

A description of the South,
That was his entire life-work,
Even though he never travelled anywhere.

Still, the navigators confirmed
The maps, the names of places, the strange customs,
Even the bird with silver claws
Which they hunted by the thousands and millions.

The King himself gave him a decoration. The ladies
Smiled nostalgically at his withered face. "It is grand,
this description", it was said,
"It is enough to make one immortal."

He smiled: "Immortality?!
Of a country? Of a city? Even this
Can sink tomorrow in the sea.
The maps, the descriptions are
A simple thought, pure coincidence."

alexandru muşina

1954-2013

New York

Nowhere does one get teary-eyed better than here.
As soon as you step into the street from the corner of your eye
The springs of oblivion gush out.
New York is the Ganges of forgetfulness.
Crazy traffic where some walk, others swim
From on high, it rains feathers which have missed their wings
Having insurance policies,
One crosses on red as on green
The traffic lights are put there simply so that we look up
Let us not forget that heaven exists
And our pedestrian crossing
Will occur suddenly
On all the colors of the rainbow
As on a zebra crossing of light.

If only once a year our past shadows
Would get out on the streets
There would be a carnival better than in Rio
Even the Work Demon wouldn't recognize us
He who licks our joints daily
Like a wild dog.

You can see what you want, believe what you wish
There is a great visual democracy
From the advertising boards in the parks
To the parks made from advertisements
To the women who smoke only on the streets
To the dogs which pull behind them

The most humanized humans.
I watch all these things with about six eyes
Two are teary due to the wind
Two from joy
And the last two, which grew later,
Put in drops of rain
So that I better see the fish of the sky
I am like a painting by Picasso
Harmoniously scattered over six canvases
If I would look at myself from a European museum
I wouldn't recognize myself anymore.

In front of me a greedy subway mouth
Swallows people seven days out of seven
On Sunday, the city wipes its mouth
With the thin sleeve of history.
From the twentieth floor on everything is rarefied
The lawyers sharpen their pencils
Directly into the helicopter blades
The pigeons find us with more difficulty
The last souls are distilled like whiskey
Through plastic tubes.
From the fiftieth floor up, the windows have a condensation
Of tear vapors
Which we have no idea how to escape.
We are alchemists made to write
We will reinvent everything, the clouds, the rain, death
And we will give them appropriate names.

1954– adrian sângeorzan

adrian sângeorzan

1954–

In Queens and Brooklyn, the immigrants
Pair up their accents
And with every child they conceive
They bring into the world a bird
Which no longer remembers the way over the ocean.

With so many skyscrapers stuck into the heavens
We appear like the beginning of a new phallic cult
A softer one, more sedate
Where "I love you"
Is like saccharin in Diet Coke
Where sex and love are substituted
And are taught in the same schools
In which the students receive
Condoms for free
And the detailed instructions for abstinence.

No one weeps here
Everyone is carrying their dreams on their shoulders
As they would a lifesaver
We are the happiest drowned people of the earth.

sunflower

Our love is dying slowly
my dear, in tardy nights
The wind wipes out our trace without resistance
And on the meadow's edge
I'll wait for you,
I'll wait to see your shadow in the distance.

The meadow's long and full
Of sunflowers in bloom,
They're present for our monumental meeting
But then the road is long
And the summer's at the end,
I have the feeling your return is fleeting…

How huge this silence now,
How hard the moon is raising
The night is cutting down on me from heavenly heights
And time erases time while waiting on,
Our love is dying slow
My dear, in tardy nights
And you don't know…

nicu alifantis

1954–

229

Ulysses (I am thinking)

marta petreu

1955–

I am thinking about you like the nymph Calypso about Ulysses
after he left on his raft for the sea voyage
towards his fate as man – therefore as a mortal
(this is Ithaca)

Just a man, like you:
house, wife, children,
a few nostalgias, a few rags, a few vows
and a dog
Oh... Those wars commanded by the gods
Or the suitors: so much manly blood and so much groaning

Remember – I tell myself – remember:
a god must be close by if there is a wound
he comes
he puts his godly mouth on the wound and sucks like a baby at the breast
he puts his godly mouth on the open wound
like unto the womanly sex
and increases his power
He moves through blood as if inside the womb

Remember – I say to myself: wherever there is pain
Whoops! The gods are there too. At least one
He sticks to pain like a leech
and stays there for times out of mind, happy as he can be
He sticks to pain like a leech until you are done

I am thinking about you like the nymph Calypso about Ulysses
after he left on the seas, on his raft towards his fate:

you, a man just like him
caught in all human things
like inside a wound

he (only the beaten leather remained)

Only the beaten leather remained

shed from pages of bodies contrived
from your heart, unbitten, like a snake
the letter S leaving me in its wake.

I am your good dog, which bites as it barks
with legs frozen still in a rock without marks

your giddy sheep with nowhere to go
its frozen legs ambushed and slow
fed from the cold mud
the fattened calf under the desert's call
returning prodigal with the sun in his thrall
the goose writing your name and mine
dipped its pen in the fat of the god at the shrine.

I am your dog, you read to him
so he goes to sleep
your jackal, your jinx
with a heart of stone
and a brain of dry gingerbread alone

your hyena killed by mercy and grace
which never wore a mark, nor a necklace too bright
found among seashells, on the witch's slick face
with a cold strand of hair
lovely and white

I am your dog
from the gates, from the fates,
to whom you read for going to sleep
between sweet thighs dark and deep
from one of the
one thousand and one deaths.

soul music

Concert
On vocal
Strings
And lutes
The song
Of life
Plays Hymns
On quiet flutes.

The song
Of animals...
That's almost
strained.
For human
Ears...
The pain,
The joy.
Defined.

1955– gabriel dumitru

The soul

However,...

Has

Its

Song...

A yearning wager:

Harmonies

Changing quickly,

Minor,

Major

A concert

Of lips...

Requires

An apology!

Of

Love...

For all

Our lives...

A eulogy.

I am smiling

Some chubby girls are looking at me
and then I realize I am smiling.
I am smiling in bus number 109 on the way to work.
of course, a good impression is impossible to make
for a long-haired young man staring through the window and smiling.
but I remembered you and, as usual, I smiled.
it is an uncontrolled reaction.
I woke up in the morning knotted in bad dreams, with skinnings alive
with knitting needles twisting my teeth
and I remembered the grammar classes.
on the bus it stinks of singlets and of petrol
and through the window what do you think? apartment blocks and
more apartment blocks.
I smiled and I was left, I believe, for some minutes with this smile on my face.
I remembered you, still in that large yellow t-shirt
and me also in a t-shirt, somewhat filthy, as we entered into the bulandra*
in the foyer, there were some stuck-up chicks
and some guys in suits...

mircea cărtărescu

1956–

---

* **Lucia Sturza Bulandra**, or simply **"the Bulandra"** – well known Bucharest theatre,
with a long tradition of promoting avant-garde, sophisticated plays.

we looked as if we landed from Woodstock,

at school, the principal started to scold me, and the secretary

threatened me

the ornamental plant un-watered on time only had about

a quarter of its foliage left

trying to regain control of the classroom

I felt the smile returning so irresistibly

that I had to turn my face towards the blackboard

1956– mircea cărtărescu

the fifth hymn
to the return of the shadow
into name and being

daniel vorona

1956–

> "Take therefore no thought for the morrow:
> for the morrow shall take thought for the things
> of itself. Sufficient unto the day is the evil thereof."
>
> (Matthew 6, 34)

: God is sad
this evening
you blind ones draw for me a loaf of bread a cup of wine
and a name of a country
here the stone does not crash into a forehead but it flies in
the middle of the circle until
it takes the form of exhaustion
and changes the color of debauchery winter
is like summer coughing in the handkerchief
an un-cadence of rain returning from the mud back to the clouds
to search for its identity
(at other times your skin was my coat thin, beneath grass of sin)
strangling my instincts, the smoke does not mean
anything anymore abstractly and lazily gliding
under the furrow seeded with tobacco and disgust
(slaves back to slavery
oxen back to the yoke
dogs back to their chains)
to the return of the shadow
into name and being

now the mountain is a lot higher on the horizontal if you turn

the valley upside down

I have come here to go away, you arrive even when you don't come

(you have legs straighter than justice)

but the indifference of your thighs is not for my renaissance

forever there's space for a new disappointment

(slaves forward in their chains

oxen forward into slavery

dogs forward in their doggedness)

p.s.

mystery light, that's what all women have been for me

from which I drank and

drank again

hemlock

thinking that I sip communion

p.p.s.

from the point of view of the storm, it remains what you squander

not what you build

as for the rest

you

know

yourself

> how much I love you, vanity of
>
> vanities

daniel vorona

1956–

matei vişniec

1956–

the horse watches over him full of sadness

I was alone in the middle of the street
under the belly of my horse
I was laying on the pavement
and my horse was looking at me, was wondering
as he had never seen me dead before

the passers-by were turning their heads a little
and looking from the corner of their eye, they were saying
how nice, the rider is dead
and the horse watches over him full of sadness

but it was not so, my horse was
just sniffing in confusion,
was trying to touch me with his damp muzzle
the passers-by were saying how nice
the rider is dead and the horse
tries to turn him face upwards

but it was not so, my horse
got bored quickly by my silence
so he left me there, on the pavement
and walked slowly along the street

landscape in a heart... beat

Into the wound's temptation fell the child,
An infant pure, on meadows running wild.
Beneath his eyelashes the heaven's resting,
The stars at dusk his thinking has beguiled.

His fragile foot sole has in it embedded
Nine flowers, seven fairy tales, three dreams,
Longing for twilight, longing, too, for sunrise,
A hawk, three shepherds, and a star which gleams.

From his dark shadow, does the light arise –
A fairy tale, a playful angel glide
The morning dew caresses him so sweetly
His palms, now scooping, and now open wide.

Deep gazing, sees this world's justification
– from whence she comes, and where she's set her goals –
And then the straw, the thorns from all the meadows,
Are on the cross, the first nails in his soles.

mihaela malea stroe

1957 –

if I hadn't been forced to speak

ioan es. pop

1958 –

if I hadn't been forced to speak,
I never would have spoken.
until I was six they did not demand it of me
and it was good like that, because I was sitting under speech
as if under a cast iron bell perfectly hermetic.

I was hiding there a science
which, at six years of age, they forced me to lose.
I was seeing the angel, not in my sleep, but verily,
in the middle of the day,
when reality is undeniable.

I never forgave them
for sending me to school,
where I had to speak,
and later, to be at pains to resemble
the others, who were speaking precipitously
while flailing their hands and legs,
making me dizzy with their life.

even to this day I only speak with dread,
because I still live there, under the bell,
and speaking makes me ill.
I have nothing to say in human speech,
where everything is happenstance and bedlam.

I pretend instead, with some dexterity,
that I speak, and outside one can hear
sounds, almost human,
but in the throat there is an illiterate and formless bellowing,
which has nothing to do with speaking.
worse is that the science of my silence is gone,
and also gone is the angel who remained
by my bedside until six years of age,
and gone is the man who could have been another man,

keeping silent in such a way that at the end
of many years of dumbness, he could have revealed
a most unforgiving science among sciences,
the only one which could have rendered death more bearable
and machines more tolerant.

1958 – ioan es. pop

life kills

my life, all of it, would fit very well inside a smaller one.

which will still have left in it, narrowly, enough space for a sheet of paper,

an inkpot and a pen.

onto which I could cling in desperation, as if to some heavy, leaden,

life-saver.

my life, all of it, could easily live inside another one, smaller.

crouched in a corner where sometime, long ago, purred a cat with a collar.

my life, all of it, would fit into a little bottle

which little angels would pass to one another,

each sipping a little pottle.

I live surrounded by things that I struggled to gather

but which are not useful to me at all.

I live to see another day, as if it was profitable in some way.

I experience wakeful nights and nightmare days rolling over me.

I wither in vain, in a haze.

surrounded by people whom I endeavored to know.

lucian vasilescu

1958 –

surrounded by people whom I'll never know.

I conduct myself among them shyly, humble in my den.

I am, from my kingdom, the last specimen.

I am visited, in the shed where I write, by nations of mice.

maybe that's what I am – one of them, one of their lot. a pest.

whose soul set long ago, weary, spent.

on a horizon where it ends even the word the end.

I am of the animal kingdom, of the male kind.

I wake up hung over each morning, to the same hospital bed confined.

and I start all over with hope and desperation.

that finally tonight, I will become some other creation.

this is why I remain watchful, and for this reason I pretend I'm alive.

this is why I pray in the wilderness.

this is why in the desert I strive.

1958– lucian vasilescu

brick up the window

since you have chosen me
make sure winter doesn't end anymore
I can't stand this indecency of nature
every broken bud hurts me
please blacken the sun
with my hollow eyes
stop the grass
this rejuvenation is humiliating

listen, the birds have not yet been strangled
the colours are running riot
my grey life seems like an invented item
as if we wouldn't be haunted by the same death

since you have chosen me
brick up that window facing the boulevard
let us love each other forlorn and ongoing
in the frozen whiteness

carmen firan

1958–

[where have you put please tell me where have you put the sun in the sky...]

***

I saw an owl writing poetry its eyes set upon the night

it was truly writing it was not an optical illusion

I saw a colt reading the poems written by me right here

below the earth where the night usually lasts

one billion and one years

I saw a nightingale wrapping its song with night

over its mouth and over its eyelids

I saw an elephant dancing with passion with an ant even

on the edge of the horizon the ant was in the day the elephant was

in the dead of midnight

I later saw a giraffe gazing at me from southward to northward

from a truly staggering height

I saw a dead tiger as well which was in tears with laughter exactly in the

middle of the night from Saturday to Sunday

I saw a fish walking on the street and it was laughing too

and its laugher was changing into night behind it

***

nicolae tzone

1958 –

unborn children

How do lost children dream?
How do they weep?
Listen for a moment, when the sun is setting,
when the wind no longer blows
and the time of evening rest is at hand,
when the voices are moving from the street
when the car engines shut up,
when the blackbirds gaze upon
the crescent moon,
when only the muddy waters
are still running through the sewers of the city
and you could hear the unborn children,
their quiet whimper...
Mindful that they do not
disrupt the peace, unborn children
only know the soothing drum-beat of the heart;

radu voinescu

1958 –

so that they do not haunt our dreams,

unborn children,

only bearing, in their closed eyes,

memories from the beginning of the world;

unborn children, unobtrusive,

letting themselves be devoured by dogs,

by hungry cats,

pecked at by birds in afternoons when the fields swelter in heat,

rotting unknown at the roots of apricot trees,

taken, in a row, towards the abyss of the sewers

drowning in a slurry of forgetfulness,

remembering, perhaps,

only the sterile chat of the doctors,

the smell of formaldehyde and

the giggle of the women who push

     the white, aseptic, prams...

the sailing boat of Trebizond

vasile ursache

1959 –

What will be left of me, beyond,
A sailing boat of Trebizond
which, in the absence of a sail,
will catch adrift a turquoise gale,
in emerald green and rubies queued
to carry to a future brood
a latent old mendacity –
phlebitis riddled rosary.
A sailing boat, a silly thimble
the flesh on deck all white and nimble,
gives you the creeps and makes you scream,
should you just spot it in a dream;
where leper sailors barely function,
while gunmen fail with consumption;
the butt of Heaven, this old boat
with rotten scaffolds, rancid bloat,
it creaks and grinds and waits for you
with silver ropes, secured askew –
pulling to break the tying thread
(nose-thumbing at the living dead!)
and chatting up a cherub sweet
who bargained, for a cent, to meet
and be its helmsman – help it fly,
to pass the straits of open sky –
that boat of Trebizond – to scam
away what's left of what I am.

… With what is left – how many times? – of what I am.

on the tram

"The tram murmurs on the tram lines. Electrical, somnolent. On the tram the air is thick like foam. You sip it, intoxicating. We the commuters, what company, are smiling, we entertain ourselves. Man, says one, isn't it good when you feel the shirt, the pants, in the morning… They are used to you, quiet, they embrace you sincerely, breezily. The tram murmurs on its lines. We fall asleep shaking slightly. On the lips of beautiful women, the butterflies stick their wings like a kiss, just so, in flight. My God, I say to a commuter, when I was a child I used to hug the pillow, a huge pillow. But I got bored of that. Now it is all quiet, it is all good. The eyelids of the tired people have grown thinner. Smile, mister commuter. It is all good. Butterflies whoosh into the engine. Electrical, somnolent. I will no longer alight at the next station. I will no longer alight."

cristian popescu

1959-1995

crowded

The tram is so crowded that the young lady in front of me is uncomfortable with my heartbeats, my heart is pushing her, is hitting her. It is the last tram. I will open the bag full of butterflies and there will be such a crush like no one ever saw before. Ah, young lady, our lips will stick together tightly, but there is nothing I can do, someone is pushing me too hard from the back. Ah, young lady, I can't be sure if this is my heartbeat or yours, but there is nothing I can do, for someone is pushing me too hard from the back. Our fingers fit in the same ring, our feet fit in the same, delicate, stiletto shoe, the young ladies fit all of them in the same dress, but there is nothing I can do, for someone pushes me too hard from the back. All the hearts beat in the chest of the tram-driver. Even he is pushed so hard from the back, that he's lost control and the tram has reached too far, in the Băneasa forest. Young lady, the butterflies lay hidden for a long time in your hair and my heart grows, grows inside your womb. Give it a girl's name, I beg you. It is late, it is quiet, and there was nothing I could do, someone pushed me too hard and this was the last tram for tonight.

prologue to the ballad of Daniel Bănulescu

I belong to the 20-30 individuals who lead the world
Timid unknown desperate
At their command posts with work desks turned
                              upside down
From the bottom of the Devil's bag
Mixed through his cello tape rolls clouds
                              and receipts
Keeping in balance the fragile language of the world
Praying without ceasing
That God includes them in the numbers of those
For whom God forgives a city
I have pulled into my prayer both my hands
                              and my feet
And I departed the world as if I tore myself
                              from a rape
Into which I was pouring my manhood
And it was me, still, holding on to the girl
In which, passing at that moment on the street
I was becoming for the third time continuously
                              guilty
I rested my forehead
On the cool window of my prayers
I remembered that:
"Whosoever shall call upon the Name of the Lord
shall be saved"
I invoked Jehovah's name and I waited
Death lives on my street
And inside my socks is death, wallowing

daniel bănulescu

1960–

Through the grass of the sex of my lover, death jumps
like a swarm of locusts
If I open my mouth on my lips death springs forth
But if I do not open it
Death continues to run inside me
As if on a happy death wall
Death is whispering to me the words
And it is death still, who prescribes to me her great
                                      healing treatments
It is death that I fear, and despite that, it is towards death
that I daily run
With my zip undone by provoking lady-like
                                      little fangs
And dancing
Right now death raised herself towards me
And laid her paws on my face and my shoulders
To sniff me lightly, but neither do I cease
                                      to pray
And almost everything earthly and real
Is like a doll with its eyes gouged and its throat slit
Reclining between death's ironic paws
From the first level of the apartment block in which I pray
My prayer flies out through the window
It cuts the anchor with which my building is tied to
                                      the ground
And the block starts to rise up into the air
                                    followed by my soul

Leaving far away

The days in which my life was carrying garbage

on its back

And observing with surprise how my prayer

Indulges in doubtful familiarity with the angels

Penetrating to the nineteenth heaven

Up there where death starts to lose its powers

And joins her voice to the voice of my prayers

Penetrating even further

Through the islands of faithful

In between the pilaf mountains of the meek

and disgusted by pilaf

In between the ardent hearts

of the doormats

Among which I tread this earth with which I cover myself

and under which I sing

I remain hanging on my prayers

Pulling deep inside my prayers

Full of some wild joy

Praying without ceasing

For God to include me

both hands and feet

in the number of those

Who dance only with the Name of their

God on their minds

And for whom God forgives a city

destinies

In my first destiny, my darling,
I was selling happiness to tourists,
as if it was fairy-floss at a crowded country-fair
– they would open their mouths wide,
take one bite,
and then throw it into the next rubbish bin.

Then, from time to time
I would suddenly transform into a chubby
Father Christmas
– always rushing with a fed up attitude –
to distribute toys made in China
to all those puerile impertinent,
many of whom deserved
a backhand across their faces.
I was whacking them now and then,
when their parents were looking away.

daniel ionita

1960–

They would scream that
Father Christmas has hit them,
but their parents would explain to them,
patiently, that
in fact, Father Christmas does not exist!

Often I would wake up as a customs officer
for thoughts and dreams,
charging duty
for all sorts of high volume subjective goods,
from prayers to palaver,
which were passing, planned or haphazardly,
through people's heads – mine, yours, everybody's.
I would stack them in a folder
to be evaluated later,
at the Last Judgment.

In the happiest of these destinies
I was becoming a nocturnal clown
with long work experience
into the amusement of your body.

daniel ionita

1960–

Finally, with the passing of time,
I was introducing myself
as a professor of calligraphy,
in a sordid world where no one
was using pens anymore.
They were all laughing at me,
pounding on keyboards -
monotonous, abject, and deadly keyboards.

But all of these destinies
flicker faintly like some lights
on the edge of the horizon,
on the edge of time,
which could not dim the brightness
of the stars in the mid-summer night sky.
Because through all of these lives
I loved you.

mona lisa

Just give me your hand, Mona Lisa, and flee;
leave moldy museums to quibble and moan –
the world waits outside, made of flesh and of bone,
with rain and with sunshine, with mountains and sea.

For hundreds of years you have hung on this wall,
in hope Leonardo will somehow appear –
while loafers and fools gave you praises or smear
and packed like sardines, they remained in your thrall.

Your gaze speaks a playful or insolent tale –
as thousands of critics are wont to explain –
but what matter words, be they wise or mundane,
when up on this wall hangs your heart, by a nail?

I'll wait till the evening at the inn down the lane,
that's crowded with people of flesh and of bone;
leave stuffy old Louvres to quibble and moan,
and we'll dance in the sunshine and run in the rain.

1960 – daniel ionita

259

call me at night

Call me at night time, but just after two
when only poetry is rising anew
and only the world remains ancient and vain
jumping around naïve and insane.
call me at night time, but just after two.

Call me at night time, but just after three
when I have just hooligans inside of me
and when the moon rays, lonely and cool
hit me and make me feel like a fool
call me at night, but just after three.

Call me at night time, but just after four
that's when the players tear up the score
and even Shakespeare can't stop them, you see…
it doesn't matter to be or not to be
call me at night time, but just after four.

Call me at night time, but just after one
as this whole craziness has just begun
and I step outside so wise and so bored,
with only a lantern instead of a sword.
call me at night time, but just after one.

You can call me at night time, whenever you like.

dinu olǎraşu

1962 –

do not touch me

do not let my palm touch you

nor my mouth cover you in deep lacerations

don't let my eyes

plunder you light

you blind, deaf and dumb man

don't step on the mine-field of my heart

at these depths

unidentified loves have committed suicide

their flesh clustered tightly around my bones

between agony and ecstasy

there is but one step

a fragile footbridge arched

over ravenous chasms

do not touch me

I died again with every new love

I have returned only to die anew.

nuţa istrate gangan

1968 –

our secret code

Do not answer, do not ask,
Lend your hand for either task,
All, to me, seems quaint, askew,
I'm so weird for loving you.

All that hasn't happened, and will never be
Doesn't rue the moment, nor eternity.
No.

Where would all the children marry, grow and spread
If today the ancients wouldn't all be dead.
All?

For the seed is loath to sprout up a new seed
If last season's grass hasn't dried indeed.
No.

What would life be like without miscalculations
One by one repeating all the irritations.
What?

andrei păunescu

1969 –

Who knows where, or whether, it will ever happen
If they build the bridge, straight or quite misshapen?
Straight?

And I keep you distant, when I draw you near
For I see you better, with my gaze unclear.
See.

Our secret code which everybody knew
Left a piece to me and left the whole to you.
Take it.

procession

the earth stays hidden behind its
little finger watching
how its inhabitants silently offer
one another the fruit of eden

erika kantor

1971–

journal 1

my life drains itself between witch hats

dizzy from the years without springtime

the snow drops have gone numb
they drained in the autumn of my eyes
absconding in silence,
seeking your iris, empty and with no answers
I find myself stuck between the indifference of time
and the hourglass within me…

erika kantor

1971–

facebook dreams (IX)

loneliness is a safe investment
makes billions on the stock exchange
produces virtual identities and merchants of masks

i want to get out from the profit sheet of those
who hunt for my loneliness
with judas' silver

i wish to remain within my list of terrors
which only God knows how to use for good

reality if more and more like a broken hourglass
from which flows a tidal wave of blood
for the lusts of a fallen angel

i am neither reality
nor deceitful mirrors

i am a dream of purification

when my love is like some kind of water

with your hands on your hips

you seem pouting a little

sweeter still

an amphora with marvelous scents

of elixirs dripping from the insides of summer

myrrh and oils

perspiration of flowers and angels

naked you draw like a deer to the edge of the forest

you pour happiness between my arms

these ablations with the mouth-water of

flowers render precisely the glassy rainbows

over the asymptotic relief of thoughts

until even my eyes had grown fingers

torn from the sun humming of the

moon living gold you flow through my

veins let us not stop

let us not stop

this whirling of the hands of the clock

at this hour

in love with itself like a dervish in

trance the hour stopped

1973– laurenţiu–ciprian tudor

the hour spiraled
out of its chain
exiled in its gliding
like a hallucinating planet
through the cosmos

let us not stop
this whirling of the hands of the clock
time outside itself
the galaxy is like a blue mayonnaise
which doesn't allow to be cut
anymore.

laurenţiu-ciprian tudor

1973-

castle

there are some children on the shore. they wish to build a castle

on the skeleton of my nothingness.

each one caresses their favorite little pebbles in their pockets. they

approach hand outstretched, look what we've found here, and laugh.

like an old ritual, they place pebbles

one by one, on my face, my breasts, my hips.

they protect me in their sunday afternoon play

and i fear that if i move, i could destroy

the edifice.

fortunately, an expected wave

bathes my cheeks – the body and the dream

come together: one step, the second,

toward the head of a cloud. the children

still laugh and gesture to me. they happily sling

their pebbles towards blue crenelated towers.

it doesn't matter

from now on i know: their dream has come true.

monica manolachi

1976–

the key

ana maria păunescu

1991–

My house shall welcome smoke from chimney burn,
And in my bed may ashes find their hiding,
While in your eyes obediently I'll turn
The key, the latches and the door that's sliding.

And from the blue, may pallid red be snowing,
The century may wilt just like a petal,
The sea may paint each wave the wind is blowing
To part, to long, to wait for snow to settle.

The edge of the abyss may prowl the street,
And thaw the glowing cinder from its ember,
While shyly you may gather at my feet
A tear, a dream, too bitter to remember.

The knell beneath the threshold may now cease,
While through our feet the cold may go to sleep,
And as for me, I promise to appease
Compendiums and birds and colors deep.

All jails and laws may jump onto the road,
The wafer and the moon, confused, may soar,
And you may choose my destiny bestowed
Onto the present and forever more.

Testament

Anthology of Romanian Verse

AUTHORS

Daniel Ionita –
editor and principal translator

"Editor and principal translator, Daniel Ionita was born in 1960 in Bucharest, Romania. Now living in Sydney, Australia, Daniel is completing his doctorate in poetry translation (Romanian to English), and teaches Organisational Improvement within the Business Practice Group – Faculty of Business at the University of Technology in Sydney. He is also the current president of the Australian-Romanian Academy for Culture. Daniel left Romania as a twenty-year old, in 1980, he lived for 10 years in Auckland, New Zealand, after which he and his family moved to Australia. Over the years he has maintained a deep interest in Romanian literature, and continues to keep in close touch with the Romanian cultural scene. He views the current volume as a tribute he owes to the country which shaped him culturally and as a person, as well as a testament which Romanian poetry endows as a gift to the culture of the world. Daniel is married, has three children, and hopes that they will read this volume."

Eva Foster – technical consultant in linguistics and poetics

"Born in 1981 in Vienna, Austria, Eva Foster is a teacher of English language and literature. Eva had, for a while, interrupted her career in order to raise her two children (Elliot and Annelise), which afforded her the necessary time to bring a valuable contribution as a linguistic and artistic consultant for this volume. Eva is now teaching full time again at Oxford Falls Grammar School on Sydney's North Shore."

Associate Professor Daniel Reynaud – technical consultant in linguistics and literature

"Born in 1958 in Armidale, New South Wales, Australia, Associate Professor Daniel Reynaud has, for a long time, been the Dean of the Faculty of Arts at Avondale College of Tertiary Education. Specialising initially in literature and the media, Daniel obtained his PhD in history, being one of the most recognised specialists in Australia's involvement in the two world wars of the twentieth century. Daniel Reynaud is widely published in this field (*The ANZAC Legend*, and *The Man the Anzacs Revered*, among others). Daniel remains close to the field of literature and creative arts."

Rochelle Bews – technical consultant in linguistics and poetics

"Born in 1979 in Invercargill, New Zealand, Rochelle Bews is a teacher of English and History who worked in Australia and the United Kingdom for 14 years. After having recently completed her MA in creative writing and literature, she is now working on her PhD which explores the freedom and potential of constrained writing."

Contents

Index

CPSIA information can be obtained
at www.ICGtesting.com
Printed in the USA
FFOW03n0142250117
31650FF

9 780995 350205